Hedges on
Hedge Funds

John Wiley & Sons

Founded in 1807, John Wiley & Sons is the oldest independent publishing company in the United States. With offices in North America, Europe, Australia, and Asia, Wiley is globally committed to developing and marketing print and electronic products and services for our customers' professional and personal knowledge and understanding.

The Wiley Finance series contains books written specifically for finance and investment professionals as well as sophisticated individual investors and their financial advisors.

Book topics range from portfolio management to e-commerce, risk management, financial engineering, valuation and financial instrument analysis, as well as much more.

For a list of available titles, visit our Web site at www.WileyFinance.com.

Hedges on
Hedge Funds

*How to Successfully Analyze
and Select an Investment*

JAMES R. HEDGES IV

WILEY

John Wiley & Sons, Inc.

Published by John Wiley & Sons, Inc., Hoboken, New Jersey.

Published simultaneously in Canada.

LJH Global Investments, LLC provides advisory services in the areas of hedge funds and alternative investments. Not all products and services are available in all locations, and not all investments are suitable for all investors.

Any discussion of investment and investment strategy of funds (including current investment themes, research and investments processes and portfolio characteristics) represents the views of LJH Global Investments, LLC as reported by the publication, at the time of publication. All expressions of opinion included herein are subject to change without notice and are not intended to be a guarantee of future events.

This book is supplied for information only and does not constitute a solicitation to buy or sell securities. Opinions expressed herein may differ from the opinions expressed by other businesses and activities of LJH Global Investments, LLC. Although information and opinions in this article have been obtained from sources believed to be reliable, LJH does not warrant the accuracy or completeness and accepts no liability for any direct or consequential losses arising from its use.

For general information on our other products and services, or technical support, please contact our Customer Care Department within the United States at 800-762-2974, outside the United States at 317-572-3993 or fax 317-572-4002.

Wiley also publishes its books in a variety of electronic formats. Some content that appears in print may not be available in electronic books.

For more information about Wiley products, visit our web site at www.wiley.com.

Library of Congress Cataloging-in-Publication Data

Hedges IV, James R., 1967–.
  Hedges on hedge funds : how to successfully analyze and select an investment / James Hedges.
     p.   cm.
  Includes index.
    ISBN 0-471-62510-8 (cloth)
  1. Hedge funds. I. Title. **MAR '07**
    HD4530.H3884 2005
    332.64′5—dc22
                                                    2004011591

Printed in the United States of America.

10 9 8 7 6 5 4 3 2 1

To Lundy, Evans, and Malone

Contents

Foreword

Does the world need another book on hedge funds? For that matter, does the world need another hedge fund? More fundamentally, does the world need another equity, convertible bond, straight bond, option, foreign exchange contract, swaption, or any of the myriad securities that underlie all hedge fund strategies? The per se answer to all of these questions is no, but the practical reality is that we will have more—much more—of all of the above. More books, more funds, more exotic combinations of securities.

Why? Because it is in the nature of markets to innovate. Because the historical record of risk-adjusted returns of the various hedge fund categories is compelling. Because the barriers to hedge fund creation are nearly nonexistent. Because there is a tidal wave of capital that wants better returns with less risk; pension funds, endowments, individuals, and even nations that have not yet supped at the hedge fund trough.

Will the marginal investor reap the risk-adjusted returns that they envision? Maybe. Will the incremental hedge fund operator succeed in providing those returns and therefore prosper? Some. Will various hedge fund strategies tend toward saturation—both by investors and practioners—thereby driving down incremental benefits? Definitely!

As the hedge fund industry enters early maturity, investors and fund managers need to look beyond the immediate imperative of producing attractive returns and contemplate the risks and opportunities in a longer time frame. We should be concerned not only with the durabilty of our strategies, but also such issues as the scalability of individual firms, strategies, and the industry; adequate disclosure and communication (transparency); the evolving regulatory environment; organizational behavior and health; and terminal value—both in terms of product offering and business economics. We need to think about the "going concern" attributes of individual funds and the industry.

As chairman of Cumberland Associates LLC, one of the longest running hedge funds on the planet, these long-term concerns are at least as important as the quotidian requirements of identifying undervalued and overvalued securities through a well-honed research process. I need to attend to the psychological and economic well being of my fellow members and staff, communicate with investors and prospects, cultivate the human and process capital that will be required for succession of ownership and management of our firm, and above all, make sure that we stay focused yet adaptable.

Central to the process of staying competent and adaptable is what I think of as a willingness to ask "dumb questions"; I have built a career on dumb questions asked of thousands of company managements, my colleagues, myself. What I am really talking about is a willingness and even a need to return constantly to fundamental issues as the context of an individual, a company, an industry, or the world evolves. My allies in this process are colleagues, both internal and external, who believe that while they know a thing or two, realize that the shelf life of an insight gets shorter every day.

For the past fifteen years, one of my most valued correspondents in this professional dialectic has been Jim Hedges. I have known him as an analyst, a client, and the proprietor of his own successful advisory and fund of fund business. Jim's hallmarks are the courage, curiosity, and confidence to think broadly, probe deeply, synthesize, and express succinctly. I have always prized his input, even when he made me squirm!

Now you too can experience the pointy end of Jim's intellect and experience. In this book, Jim has posed the "dumb" and sophisticated questions that all investors and investment managers should be asking themselves and has set forth his thoughts for our benefit. But this work is more than a compilation of his own observations and opinions; he has called upon commentators and practitioners who have earned his respect to broaden and deepen this offering.

The utility of this book to the hedge fund investor, particulary the novice, is readily apparent. I happen to think that it should be required reading for the hedge fund professional as well. One of the salient weaknesses of the hedge fund industry is the predominance of the "sole-proprietor" model, in which one personality dominates the deployment of capital. This structure inherently lacks strong checks and balances. If this sounds like your firm you should read this book.

Investors need to recognize that the combination of low barriers to entry and lucrative returns has attracted thousands of new hedge fund proprietors. Investors have exhibited a fairly marked tendency to try to discover "hot" new managers; have overemphasized facile quantitative measures of risk; have underemphasized qualitative, ethical, and structural elements of managers; and have unrealistically projected short or nonexistent performance records. In so doing, they have often incurred much greater risk and/or disappointing returns than they expected.

The explosion in new hedge fund capital is coinciding with broadening distribution and access. The offerings will reach marginally less sophisticated investors—be they institutions or individuals—as the overall probability of gaining "excess" returns diminishes for the hedge fund universe as a whole. The rate of innovation, number of vehicles, and risks in the hedge fund world will proliferate at an ever faster pace. It is incumbent upon investors to educate and protect themselves; this book is an excellent place to start or revew that education.

Bruce G. Wilcox, Chairman
Management Committee,
Cumberland Associates LLC

Preface

The bull market of the late 1990s created significant wealth, yet subsequent bear market years diminished many investor portfolios. Naturally, investors find the concept of shrinking assets to be unacceptable and seek ways to generate greater wealth. Emulating the best practices of the world's most successful investors has led to increasing "retailization" of hedge funds, funds that formerly were available only to the world's richest individuals.

Although hedge funds are not yet sold at the corner bank branch or ATM, that is not beyond the realm of possibility. The industry continues to experience exponential growth with studies predicting $4 trillion in hedge fund assets by 2010—up from close to $800 billion in 2004. (See Figure P.1.) Because hedge fund investing is based on a dynamic approach that is uncorrelated to general market conditions, its appeal continues to expand and more investors than ever seek ways to capitalize on the hedge fund opportunity. As a result, there are more hedge funds around than ever, a number of new products, and increasing confusion.

Indeed, hedge fund investing is a complicated task even for those with substantial resources or investment experience. The hedge fund industry is rife with both deliberate mystification and legitimate complexity. This book demystifies hedge funds and clarifies the built-in complexities to enable more investors to introduce, in a prudent manner, absolute return-oriented investment strategies and vehicles into their overall investment program.

Misconceptions regarding hedge fund investing stem largely from high-profile stories about large, highly secretive and speculative hedge

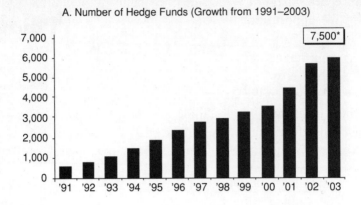

A. Number of Hedge Funds (Growth from 1991–2003)

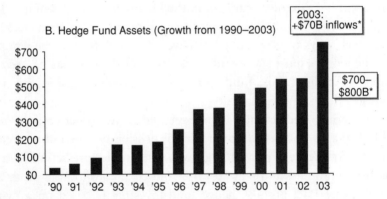

B. Hedge Fund Assets (Growth from 1990–2003)

FIGURE P.1   The historical growth of hedge funds.
Source: Hedge Fund Research, Inc.
*Approximate industry estimations

funds that either blew up or made a bundle on a multibillion-dollar gamble, in either instance taking down a national economy or two as a result. But as the hedge fund industry has grown and evolved, the headlines and the stories that followed have taken on a lot more of the substance and nuance required to do justice to the complexities of hedge funds and the hedge fund industry. Figure P.2 presents a history of the hedge fund market.

Although scandalous headlines still show up with disturbing regularity, it is increasingly common to see stories that report on the real substance behind the dramatic growth of hedge funds: the growing demand for opportunities to pursue absolute as opposed to relative investment returns.

This book summarizes what hedge funds are and how they can help us all to make more money. Most important, it looks at where the industry is headed and what smart investors need to do now to accomplish their investment goals. Table P.1 shows the difference in risk between hedge funds and more "traditional" investments.

Chapter 1 outlines the hedge fund alternative, including the basic attributes of hedge funds, the major strategies they use to pursue their investment objectives, the comprehensive process of manager evaluation and selection, and some of the complexities associated with hedge fund investing through what is known as a fund of funds (FOFs) or fund of hedge funds (FOHFs).

Chapter 2 explores how to cut through the black box and timely issues related to hedge fund disclosure and transparency, which is the degree to which investors and/or regulators can or should be informed

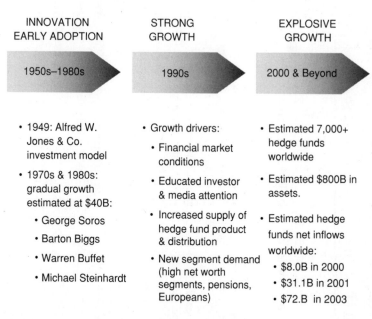

Figure P.2   History of the hedge fund market.

TABLE P.1 Key Differences in Risk between Hedge Funds and "Traditional" Investments

	Hedge Funds	Traditional Investment Portfolios	Implication
Investment styles	Defining characteristic. Vary substantially.	Vary moderately.	• Investor must map risk. • Cross-style, -manager aggregation of risk are difficult.
Exposure to market	Varies from multiples of − 1 (short seller with leverage) to + 1 (long-bias with leverage).	All sector/style indices have β to the market of around 1.	• Manager "skill" important. • "Process risk" more relevant.
Standard format to measure/report risk	None: different hedge funds map risk differently, often use derivatives.	Well established—can map mutual fund risks/returns onto standard asset classes.	• Requires detailed individual examination of funds.
Value at Risk (VaR)	Limited value: VaR measures differ widely across managers.	Of great value—time horizons, confidence levels, asset mixes generally comparable.	• Risk analysis applied to long-only managers insufficient for hedge fund managers.
Risk profiles	Differ considerably: − e.g., take credit risk.	Well-defined risk profiles, analytics.	• Investor as "global risk manager"—manages risk selects funds with different styles, exposures.

Liquidity crisis risk	Vulnerable—exacerbated to extent use leverage, less liquid markets/instruments/style.	Equally vulnerable—can affect hedge funds and long-only manager equally.	• Quantification of *interplay* of liquidities, risk, leverage, styles, etc., is critical.
Performance data	Subject to a number of risk biases.	Subject to far fewer biases.	• Risk of inflated expectations. • Requires sophisticated due diligence and monitoring.
Sharpe ratio	Partially applicable—but does not fully capture hedge fund nonlinearity.	Fully applicable—developed for long-only "linear" investments.	• Requires detailed individual examination of funds.
Short volatility bias	Short options exposure can boost Sharpe ratio, leading to overallocation, higher risk.	Limited, if any, options shorting.	• Risk of overallocation. • Scrutinize high Sharpe. • Scrutinize use of short options.
Interplay of risks	Not only the greater variety of risk but, critically, their overall interplay drives risk-adjusted returns.	Market risk—equity, interest rate, and credit risk—drive risk-adjusted returns.	• Must scrutinize risk in aggregate. • "Intelligent" diversification is critical.

about a fund's actual investments and investment practices. Current transparency issues relate to both investor demand for increased transparency and pending regulations, which are prompting hedge funds to dramatically rethink approaches to this issue.

Chapter 3, written by two principals from LJH's partner company, Capco, underscores the challenges involved in due diligence and portfolio monitoring by relating the findings of a comprehensive study of over 10 years of hedge fund blow-ups. Investors will learn more about what to watch out for when making a hedge fund investment decision.

Chapter 4 focuses on the single largest category of hedge fund fraud, improper valuation of portfolio holdings. It outlines the red flags investors need to watch out for and tells investors why valuation is a potential "industry black eye" they need to monitor.

Chapter 5 delves into the issue of size versus performance in the hedge fund industry, a study that points to the need for investors to evaluate managers of all sizes when making hedge fund allocations.

Chapter 6 looks at two fast-growing directional strategies, the global macro strategy and managed futures investing, and outlines how investors can profit from the global economic markets and commodities trading.

Chapter 7 is an overview of distressed securities and merger arbitrage, two of the principal event-driven strategies that present investors with an opportunity to profit from events that occur during the corporate life cycle.

Chapter 8 covers two prominent nondirectional or relative value strategies, convertible bond arbitrage and fixed income arbitrage.

Chapter 9 delves into a third relative value strategy, equity market neutral, which helps investors profit in either up or down markets.

Chapter 10 looks at technology sector investing and how this volatile and dynamic investment sector can lead to profits.

Chapter 11 begins a discussion of geographic sector investing by looking in the current prospects for investing in Europe, a region whose level of international prominence is expanding.

Chapter 12 examines investment opportunities in Asia, where investors have an opportunity to take advantage of Japan's tumultuous market, rule changes, and volatility.

Chapter 13 looks at hedge fund indices, including the new investable indices, and helps investors to understand how to track with reasonable confidence the directionality of hedge fund performance.

The glossary contains commonly used hedge fund terms aimed at clarifying oft-used words in the industry.

Before we begin, however, I want to give you a sense of my own background, how I developed my particular take on the world of hedge funds, and why I approach this introduction to the industry a little differently from how others might.

For over a decade now, I have been the president and chief investment officer of LJH Global Investments, an investment advisory firm founded with a focus on introducing the benefits of absolute return investing to high-net-worth individuals, institutions, and their advisors through the creation of custom tailored hedge fund portfolios.

From the beginning, the LJH approach has been to identify and provide access to top hedge fund managers who have passed a rigorous due diligence conducted by a team of hedge fund research analysts who specialize by individual strategy. During the last 10-plus years, we have helped some of the world's wealthiest families invest in hedge funds and have established ourselves as a leading global hedge fund advisory firm called on by financial services firms as a subadvisor to build, manage, and service FOHF products. We also have served as direct advisors to pension funds, family offices, and other high-net-worth individuals in the construction of individual hedge fund portfolios, and have provided FOHFs products for direct distribution to qualified investors. Our firm was one of the first to develop fund of hedge funds registered with the Securities and Exchange Commission (SEC), an insurance clone product, and an array of structured hedge fund products.

I want to make two points about how this background has both motivated me to write this book and influenced its content.

First, this book is the logical outcome of LJH's commitment to thought leadership in the hedge fund industry, stemming from a belief in the fundamental importance of promoting realistic expectations regarding hedge funds as an asset class. This commitment has been expressed in several ways and in a variety of forums. For over a decade, LJH has hosted an annual client summit where many of the best minds in the industry gather to discuss and debate timely issues of importance to investors. LJH speakers also address industry issues at investment conferences and before regulatory agencies in the United States and abroad. In 2002 I was the first fund of hedge funds expert ever invited to speak to executives from the Bank of Japan. In the spring of 2003 I was one of the experts invited to testify before the SEC in its most recent reexamination of the hedge fund industry.

In addition to the ongoing publication of a series of thought-provoking and practical white papers on a range of industry issues, LJH experts are also sought out for commentary by financial publications including *Forbes, Institutional Investor,* the *New York Times, Barron's,* and the *Wall Street Journal,* and have appeared on business television shows including CNN, CNBC, and Bloomberg. Outstanding product development combined with these robust, ongoing investor education activities are the keys to thought leadership in our industry.

Second, this book strives to provide the reader with a wealth of information that can be put to practical use. Much of this information is representative of the intelligence that our firm has gleaned from leading hedge fund managers and others within the industry. Making a hedge fund investment is very much an act of trust, and judgment regarding the character of managers to whom one might entrust a significant portion of one's assets is perhaps the most practical element in the entire investment allocation process.

Acknowledgments

This book is a compilation of many of our firm's best ideas and would not be possible without the talented team of people who have worked with us through the years. Thank you also to all of the LJH clients for whose hedge fund investing journey we have managed and to the other friends of LJH who have contributed to our firm's success. I would also like to thank the numerous hedge fund managers with whom I have spent countless hours over the years. Your stories, firms, expertise, and success are the foundation of our business. Most of all, I wish to express my greatest appreciation to my partner, Charlotte Luer, without whose support, creativity, and energy this book would have never materialized.

Hedges on
Hedge Funds

CHAPTER 1

The Hedge Fund Alternative

SUCCESSFUL INVESTING REQUIRES KNOWLEDGE

The first step in being a successful investor in hedge funds or other types of investments is getting in the driver's seat and learning everything you can about timely opportunities and how they mesh with your objectives. Cruising along, pursuing the same investment philosophy that you have used for years, is certainly an option, and if you are achieving the returns you want, that is a wise road to follow. However, if you are like most investors, it is likely your investment process could use a boost. Exploring the addition of hedge funds to your portfolio is a good use of your time and effort, and you are smart to learn everything you can about this asset class.

What exactly is a hedge fund? For years, hedge funds have been the subject of cocktail party talk and an oft-discussed subject for news articles and business shows. Unfortunately, most investors do not really understand hedge funds or how they differ from traditional stock and bond investments. One of the common comments is that hedge funds are risky, a belief fueled by misconceptions and a lack of understanding in the area. For instance, the very meaning of "hedge" implies reducing risk. Hedge funds continue to spark the curiosity of investors, yet with that curiosity comes a need to better understand the industry and its respective strategies. Before thinking about whether to invest in hedge funds, investors need a clear understanding of what a hedge fund is, what it is not, and how it works. (See Table 1.1.)

TABLE 1.1   Overall Objectives of Alternative Investments

- Preservation of captial
- Wealth accumulation/growth
- Management of risk and volatility
- Enhanced returns
- Low correlation/diversification
- Access to strategies unavailable to traditional managers

Basically, hedge funds are considered to be a type of alternative investment, along with venture capital and private equity funds, real estate, and commodities. (See Figure 1.1.) The term "hedge fund" is derived from the practice of investment managers who took long positions in various securities and then hedged against the risk of a general market decline by taking short positions in other securities. In practice, the term has a much broader usage, generally referring to private investment vehicles that, by availing themselves of certain exemptions allowed in current securities laws, may utilize a wide range of investment strategies and instruments.

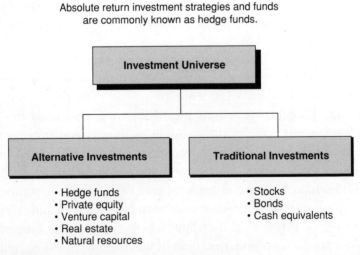

FIGURE 1.1   Alternative Investment Strategies.

In the simplest, formal terms, hedge funds are little more than commingled pools of capital structured as limited partnerships, limited liability corporations, or offshore investment companies, offered exclusively via private placements to a relatively limited number of accredited investors who meet certain predetermined qualifications set forth in federal securities laws. These laws provide strict criteria for those eligible to invest in hedge funds. Hedge funds require that at least 65 of their 99 allowed investors be accredited, as defined as an individual or couple with a net worth of at least $1 million, or an individual who had an annual income in the previous two years of at least $200,000 ($300,000 for a couple). In reality, a potential hedge fund investor needs more than that to be fully diversified and qualify to meet the fund's minimum investment requirements. Minimum requirements range from $250,000 to $10 million, and the most common ones range between $500,000 and $1 million. New regulations allow for up to 499 investors per hedge fund as long as all the investors are qualified purchasers, which are defined as individuals with at least a $5 million liquid net worth. (See Table 1.2.)

Securities laws also regulate how hedge funds may obtain assets. Hedge funds are not allowed to engage in any form of public solicitation of funds but can acquire funds only through means of completely private introductions or existing relationships. The thinking behind

TABLE 1.2 Traditional versus Hedge Funds

	Traditional	Hedge Funds
Performance objectives	Relative returns	Absolute returns
Investment vehicles	Stocks, bonds, cash	All asset classes/vehicles
Investment strategies	Limited	Wide range
Regulation structure	Regulated	Largely unregulated
Performance drivers	Asset class and market correlation	Fund manager skill
Fees	Management fee only, rarely performance incentive	Management fee plus performance incentive fee
Liquidity	Unrestricted, often daily	Restricted

these regulations is that such investors are sophisticated enough to understand the kinds of investment techniques a hedge fund manager may employ and thus appreciate and withstand the kinds of risks being taken. However, these two components of the regulatory structure help to foster an image of the industry as exclusive, elite, and secretive. The Securities and Exchange Commission (SEC) currently is reviewing the subject of hedge fund marketing as part of its ongoing review of hedge funds; investors may see changes to these rules in the coming years.

Another significant defining attribute of hedge funds deals with the fees charged. In contrast to traditional long-only investment managers, most hedge fund managers charge their clients an incentive fee in addition to a standard management fee. The most common fee structure includes an annual management fee of 1 percent of assets under management and 20 percent of the net annual return. Much of the continued strong growth of the hedge fund industry stems from this factor alone. Because of the potential to earn significantly more money as a hedge fund manager than as an employee of a large financial institution, the motivation to start and manage a hedge fund is compelling. Indeed, large, successful hedge fund managers can earn multimillion-dollar salaries, and clients typically do not mind paying high performance fees when the manager is achieving strong, justifiable results.

The investment industry has come to use the term "alpha" (in distinction to "beta," referring to the normal return of any given market or security) to refer to both the ability of a manager to outperform a benchmark and to the degree of outperformance itself.

Thus, it is helpful to think of a hedge fund as an investment vehicle where the preponderance of the return comes from the skill of the trader rather than the return of the markets. Although not without disadvantages, this arrangement is generally accepted as an essential dynamic of hedge fund performance and worth the price for superior investment returns.

HEDGE FUND DISTINCTIONS

Several other attributes differentiate hedge funds from other investment vehicles.

Investment Strategies

Traditional investment advisors are limited in their investment options, whereas alternative investment advisors are opportunistic. Alternative investment managers can take larger position sizes, invest across asset classes and security types, and employ strategies whose returns generally come from the exploitation of market inefficiencies, not market movements. Alternative investment strategies are also dynamic by nature. Fund managers can use leverage and sell securities short to vary market exposure actively. Alternative investment returns are therefore a product of how the manager invests, not just where the manager invests.

Return Objectives

The concept of absolute versus relative returns is central to the alternative investment sector. Unlike traditional investment managers driven by index weightings, nontraditional managers invest for absolute returns, not returns relative to the broad market. Most of the returns from alternative investment strategies come from the skill of the manager rather than the returns of an asset class. Table 1.3 presents characteristics of hedge fund strategies.

Minimum Investment Requirements

For the most part, due to the limited number of clients who can be invested in a fund, the minimum investments steadily increase as the years go by. A manager's initial minimum may be as low as $250,000 or $500,000, but can quickly increase by a multiple. There is no shortage of tier 1 investment managers who have minimum requirements in excess of $10 million. As institutions play an increasing role in the alternative investment arena, fund managers often are induced to take on as clients institutions rather than private individuals who, in most cases, allocate substantially smaller amounts.

Coinvestment Opportunities

Hedge fund managers tend to invest a significant portion of their own capital in their partnerships, thereby reinforcing their commitment to

TABLE 1.3 Hedge Fund Strategy Characteristics

Category	Substrategy	Risk[a]	Volatility	Correlation[b]
Relative Value/Market Neutral	Convertible arb Fixed-income arb Equity market neutral	Low	Low	Low
Event Driven	Merger arbitrage Distressed securities Special situations	Medium	Low	Low
Equity Hedge (L/S)	Long/short Short selling	Medium to high	Medium to high	Variable
Global Macro (Tactical)	Global macro Managed futures/CTAs Emerging markets	High	Very high	No to negative
Fund of Hedge Funds	Strategy specific Sector specific	Low	Low-moderate can vary according to ratio of funds and strategy	Low

Category	Leverage[c]	Focus	(Non)/Directional	Return Attribution
Relative Value/Market Neutral	High 3:1 to 5:1	Exploit pricing inefficiencies Neutralize L/S positions Minimize directional effect	Non	Consistence and diversification
Event Driven	Low 2:1 or less	Exploit unrealized value Transaction and time-driven	Non	Increased adjustment of risk
Equity Hedge (L/S)	Low 2:1 or less	Combine L/S equity and bonds to reduce market exposure and isolate performance while managing portfolio risk	Directional	Enhancer Risk reducer
Global Macro (Tactical)	Variable 2:1–5:1	Opportunistic, aggressive posturing Exploitation of macroeconomic trends One-way speculation on future movements	Directional	Enhancer Risk reducer
Fund of Hedge Funds	Low-moderate	Stock diversification and long term stabilization of returns Seeks preservation of capital in down markets while capturing alpha in up markets	Non	Seeks consistency and predictability

[a]Note that this level is an overall, generalized risk assignment for the category; there will be varying levels of risk within each substrategy.
[b]With traditional markets
[c]Average range.

their fund's performance. This aspect differs greatly from the world of traditional investment advisors where, for regulatory reasons, managers often are discouraged from purchasing their own proprietary product.

Liquidity

Unlike managed accounts or mutual funds, alternative investment vehicles may typically require a lock-up of 12 months before withdrawals are permitted. Some offshore funds offer liquidity as frequently as weekly, but certain onshore long-term investment pools may require commitments of up to 4 years. It is important to make sure that the fund's liquidity constraints are in keeping with industry norms for the strategy employed.

Access and Transparency

The limited partnership format provides the manager with flexibility to deliver returns that would not be possible through other formats, but it also obscures a client's ability to monitor investment activities. Furthermore, many managers are hesitant to allow clients to second-guess their judgment in short-term increments. Without special considerations, it can be exceedingly difficult to monitor whether a manager is diverging from the stated strategy, inappropriately using derivatives or leverage, or engaging in other unacceptable behavior.

Beyond the formal characteristics of what defines a hedge fund, how do hedge funds actually attempt to pursue their investment objectives? Although there are several competing ways to classify and name the many hedge fund styles and strategies, three broad categories should be useful for introductory purposes: (1) directional, (2) nondirectional, and (3) event-driven/opportunistic.

DIRECTIONAL STRATEGIES

This category includes those funds seeking returns based on trend-following trades or market directional investments that may be hedged or unhedged. Global macro, long/short strategies, and short selling are typical directional strategies.

Global Macro

Perhaps the most prominent of the directional strategists are the global macro managers. These institutional managers run large and highly diversified portfolios designed to profit from major shifts in global capital flows, interest rates, and currencies. Commodity trading advisors also are placed into this category if they are running a nondiscretionary, or systems trading, program. Global macro funds represent the purest form of a top-down approach to hedge fund investing. The primary strategy of the macro fund managers is an opportunistic approach based on shifts in global economies. Global macro managers speculate on changes in countries' economic policies and shifts in currency and interest rates via derivatives and the use of leverage. Portfolios tend to be highly concentrated in a small number of investment themes, and typically place large bets on the relative valuations of two asset categories. Global macro managers structure complex combinations of investments to benefit from the narrowing or widening of the valuation spreads between these assets in such a way as to maximize the potential return and minimize potential losses. In some instances, the investments are designed specifically to take advantage of artificial imbalances in the marketplace brought on by central bank activities.

Long/Short Strategies

Long/short funds constitute in aggregate the largest single approach to hedge fund investing. This strategy involves investing in equity and/or bond markets combining long investments with short sales to reduce, but not eliminate, market exposure and isolate the performance of the fund from the performance of the asset class as a whole. Returns can be more correlated with other asset classes due to bias toward long market exposure. Hedged equity funds invest both long and short and adjust the ratio of the long and short positions to capitalize on market trends. Financial leverage is used to varying degrees depending on the manager's investment process. Options, futures, and derivative securities also can be used either to hedge (i.e., control risk) or to enhance returns by providing additional leverage. Long/short funds can be categorized further by geography or sector, although due to particularities of either certain geographies or industry sectors, they also might be more appropriately considered opportunistic.

Short Selling

Short sellers are the ultimate directional managers because they take bets on a market downturn. This strategy is based on the sale of securities that are believed to be overvalued from either a technical or a fundamental viewpoint. The investor does not own the shares sold, but instead borrows them from a broker in anticipation that the share price will fall and that the shares may be bought later at a lower price to replace those borrowed from the broker earlier. Short sellers typically focus on situations in which they believe stock prices are being supported by unrealistic expectations. Misleading accounting practices and managerial fraud result in some of the most profitable investments. One risk unique to short selling is the short squeeze, in which buyers drive prices up to force the short sellers to cover their positions.

NONDIRECTIONAL STRATEGIES

Nondirectional strategies are not dependent on the direction of any specific market and are commonly called specific forms of arbitrage, market-neutral, or relative value investing. In other words, these strategies seek to effectively neutralize market influences and to profit only from capturing the difference in price between two related securities. Because the price discrepancies these funds seek to capture are generally quite small, these funds often can involve the use of large amounts of financial leverage. Some of the principal strategies in this category include:

- Convertible arbitrage
- Fixed-income arbitrage
- Income arbitrage
- Closed-end fund arbitrage
- Equity market neutral

Convertible Arbitrage

Convertible arbitrageurs are simultaneously long the convertible securities and short the underlying equities of the same issuer, thereby working the spread between the two types of securities. Returns result from the difference between cash flows collected through coupon payments and short interest rebates and cash paid out to cover dividend payments on the short equity positions. Returns also can result from the convergence of valuations between the two securities. Risk originates from the widening of the valuation spreads due to rising interest rates or changes in investor preference. The focus of investments can be nation-specific or global in nature. Convertible arbitrage generally is considered a relatively conservative strategy with moderate expected volatility. Certain managers, however, have chosen to enhance the expected return by leveraging their holdings, which also can increase volatility, depending on how the positions are structured.

Fixed-Income Arbitrage

Fixed-income arbitrage involves taking long and short positions in bonds and other interest-rate-sensitive securities. These positions, when combined, approximate one another in terms of rate and maturity but for some reason are suffering from pricing inefficiencies. Risk varies with the types of trades and level of leverage employed. In the United States, this strategy often is implemented through mortgage-backed bonds and other mortgage derivative securities. This strategy has proven to be a very profitable but unpredictable one. Mortgage securities carry embedded options that are very difficult to value and even more difficult to hedge. Many managers have found attractive opportunities overseas, but typically they are reticent to disclose the specific nature of their trades. Portfolio disclosure in this strategy is often nonexistent.

Index Arbitrage

Index arbitrage involves buying or selling a basket of stocks or other securities and taking a counter position in index futures contracts or options to capture differentials due to inefficiencies in the market. Unfortunately, computerized trading and the massive liquidity of modern securities markets have conspired to increase the efficiency of index pricing and therefore reduce the potential for profits from this strategy. Very few fund managers participate in the index arbitrage market. Most index arbitrage investors are trading proprietary capital. Therefore, accurate expected return data are not available.

Closed-End Fund Arbitrage

Closed-end fund arbitrage, like stock index arbitrage, involves buying or selling a basket of stocks, which in this case replicates the holdings of a closed-end mutual fund. The key to the process is identifying closed-end mutual funds that are trading at prices substantially different from their net asset value and will correct to a more normal valuation in the future. Closed-end mutual funds are less liquid than indexes and less transparent as to their holdings. They therefore represent a less efficiently valued security class, which presents greater opportunity, but also greater potential risk than index arbitrage. Closed-end fund arbitrage is rarely practiced as a stand-alone strategy. Accurate expected return data are therefore not available.

Equity Market-Neutral Strategies

Equity market-neutral strategies invest in a range of equity and equity-derivative securities using complicated quantitatively intensive models designed to hedge away virtually all market risk.

EVENT-DRIVEN AND OPPORTUNISTIC STRATEGIES

The event-driven category includes those funds that seek to capitalize on price fluctuations or imbalances stemming from a specific event occurring during the life cycle of a corporation, such as a merger, bankruptcy, corporate restructuring, or spin-off. This category can be broken down into four specific strategies: (1) distressed securities, (2) risk (merger) arbitrage, (3) special situations, and (4) sector funds. The individual strategies within event-driven investing can be employed individually or simultaneously, depending on the investment process of the individual manager. These strategies also could be classified as nondirectional instruments inasmuch as the outcome is largely dependent on company-specific issues that have little or no correlation to market movements.

Other opportunistic strategies encompass a range of niche strategy specialists who offer the ability to capitalize on shorter-term inefficiencies. These managers frequently work in highly distressed, newly developed, or otherwise inefficiently priced markets or sectors. Due to the reduced liquidity inherent in many such situations, these managers frequently run smaller pools of capital than their institutional counterparts. Examples of opportunistic strategies are microcap stocks (often called small cap or sector funds).

Distressed Securities

Sometimes referred to as vulture investors, distressed securities managers typically invest long and short in the securities of companies undergoing bankruptcy or reorganization. Managers tend to focus on companies that are undergoing financial rather than operation distress—in other words, good companies with bad balance sheets. Overleveraged companies that are unable to cover their debt burden become oversold as institutional bondholders liquidate their holdings. As the companies enter bankruptcy, distressed securities managers buy the positions at pennies on the dollar. Managers often become actively involved in the workout process and frequently have in-house legal teams to fight for advantageous treatment of their class. Some distressed securities managers also invest in the equity securities issued at the end of the bankruptcy proceedings. These securities, called stub equities, often are overlooked by traditional investment managers. Other distressed securities funds have moved into the loan origination business. These funds approach the market with a more creative attitude than traditional lenders and are willing to do the work to accurately appraise unusual types of collateral. The loans are typically shortterm, highly collateralized, and very expensive. Lending rates typically start at 15 percent. Although commonly viewed as a risky investment, volatility actually varies with the strategies employed and the securities held. Volatility of returns is greatest among those managers investing in high-yield debt and postbankruptcy stub equities. Lower-volatility investments include late-stage investing in senior secured debt. This strategy typically does not use financial leverage.

Risk Arbitrage

Risk arbitrage (also called merger arbitrage) managers take a long position in the stock of a company being acquired in a merger, leveraged buyout, or takeover and a simultaneous short position in the stock of the acquiring company. If the takeover fails, this strategy may result in large losses. Often risk is reduced by avoiding hostile takeovers and by investing only in deals that are announced. In recent years the spreads between the prices of the stocks of companies involved in these transactions have reached all-time lows. The potential profit spreads between the initial offers and the final deal prices are greatest in hostile transactions. Most transactions announced today are friendly, and, in the case of unsolicited offers, the initial bids often are very close to the final number. To overcome this problem, many risk arbitrage managers are increasing the risk profile of their portfolios, which is evidenced by an increased level of leverage and greater net-long exposures.

Special Situations

Event-driven managers can take advantage of special situations with a significant position in the equity of a firm. Many special-situation investments cross over into distressed securities investments and risk arbitrage. However, special-situation managers tend to focus on new or underfollowed areas of opportunity, such as emerging market debt, depressed stock, impending (i.e., unannounced) mergers/acquisitions, reorganizations, and emerging bad news that may temporarily devalue stock prices. Typically leverage is not employed. The nature of the investments made involves greater volatility than the other event-driven strategies.

Sector Funds

Sector funds represent a top-down approach to investing within the domestic hedge fund category. Sector funds invest long and short in the companies of specific sectors of the economy. Examples of such sector specialization include technology companies, financial institutions, healthcare and biotech companies, electrical utility companies, real estate investment trusts (REITs), entertainment and communications companies, gold stocks, and energy companies. Managers construct portfolios of long and short positions based on a research-intensive process.

Why should investors consider hedge funds? The facts speak for themselves. The differences between alternative and traditional investments are manifested in historical returns, and alternative investment strategies outperformed traditional investments on a risk/return basis from 1994 to 2000. Despite the Standard & Poor's (S&P) 500 slightly outperforming hedge funds on an average annual return basis from 1994 through 2000 due to the market's unprecedented bull run, hedge funds still averaged more than 15 percent annual returns over the period. When the time period is expanded to include all years since 1989, hedge funds have outperformed the S&P on an average return basis as well as 50 percent better on a risk-adjusted basis. When the subsequent bear market years of 2000 to 2002 are included, hedge funds outperformed the S&P 500 on both an absolute and a risk-adjusted basis.

In addition to outright performance, hedge funds also can significantly reduce the overall risk of a portfolio because of the low correlation of these fund types with the market and among hedge fund categories. A study by Duke University researchers indicated that more than half of all mutual funds have a correlation to the market of greater than 75 percent; typical hedge funds have a much lower correlation with the market. The low correlations of alternative investments can make them an ideal diversification tool for any portfolio. Modern theory states that adding a noncorrelated, volatile investment to a portfolio can reduce the overall volatility. Adding alternative investments to a traditional equity and fixed-income portfolio reduces overall portfolio volatility, and the end result is a substantially greater risk-adjusted return.

For a predetermined level of risk (standard deviation), a portfolio including hedge funds has the potential to deliver a higher risk-adjusted return to the overall portfolio. (See Table 1.4.)

Investing in hedge funds requires a determination of the appropriate portfolio allocation and the identification of strategies in which one seeks to invest. The first step in investing in a hedge fund is the same as in making any other investment decision: determining the individual investor's overall objectives by specifying as clearly as possible both return requirements and risk tolerance. After a full consideration of the investor's time horizon, tax considerations, liquidity constraints, regula-

TABLE 1.4   Unique Return and Risk-Reduction Opportunities of Hedge Fund Strategies

---

- Hedge funds are *not* necessarily riskier than many traditional stocks and bond investments.
- Hedge funds can add benefits to establish traditional asset portfolios through:
  - ☐ Enhanced risk-adjusted returns
  - ☐ Diversification/low correlation to traditional investments
  - ☐ Access to investment strategies cannot get elsewhere
  - ☐ Access to some of the top asset managers in the world

---

tion, and other circumstances unique to the investor, one then can formulate an investment policy that will allocate funds in the most appropriate fashion. This process includes specifying the asset classes to be included in the portfolio, determining capital market expectations, deriving the most effective alternative portfolios, and funding the optimal asset mix. In making specific alternative investment decisions, one should always try to have realistic expectations about how any given investment contributes to achieving one or more of only three ultimate reasons to invest in hedge funds: return enhancement, risk reduction, or specific investment opportunities that are otherwise unavailable.

IDENTIFICATION OF MANAGERS

Because of restrictions on advertising, identifying potential hedge funds with which to invest is challenging. The most common way to select funds is to consult one or more of several commercially available directories or databases. The challenge then becomes one of narrowing the field to a manageable number that deserve further attention. At this point, investors can apply set criteria and come up with a list of items to investigate in greater detail. However, it is critical to keep in mind that these resources are useful only as a starting point because of several limitations to the kind of data they contain and the quality of that data. The principal flaw of databases is that they tend to offer little more than purely quantitative and historical information. More specifically, data integrity can be problematic due to the different sources these databases rely on to get their information. For instance, a comparison of the leading hedge fund databases will uncover substantial disparities in managers' historical performances. Last, many managers are reluctant to allow information about their funds to be published. According to SEC officials, publication of such information, even by an unaffiliated firm, may constitute unlawful advertisement. The result is that some of the best firms remain unlisted and essentially invisible to the general public; thus they can be accessed only (if they are even open to additional funds) through a direct introduction.

Nevertheless, with these limitations in mind, the process of identifying managers essentially involves developing a set of screening criteria to apply to a broad universe of funds contained in a directory or database. From the resulting list one can move on to the remaining steps in pursuing a hedge fund investment.

EVALUATION OF MANAGERS

After initially identifying potential funds with which to invest, a further layer of specialized due diligence is needed. The four main elements of a successful evaluation process are:

1. Collection and analysis of partnership documents
2. Quantitative analysis of returns
3. Background and reference checks
4. On-site interviews

Analysis of Disclosures

The limited partnership structure of most hedge funds provides investment flexibility, but also poses significant challenges to the due diligence process. It is crucial for family office professionals to develop the unique tools necessary for evaluating funds based on their investment strategies, personnel, and general business plans. If the family office chooses not to develop this expertise in-house, engaging an alternative investment professional should be considered the price of entry to these investments.

Quantitative Analysis

Sophisticated computer programs often are used in the manager evaluation process. Analysis of the returns provides data that can be used to compare various strategies and managers based on risk/return measures as well as the correlation of returns. However, quantitative analysis should not be used as a crutch in place of sound qualitative analysis. The simplicity of transforming art into science provides investors with a false sense of security. Further, the utility of statistical analysis is completely dependent on the extrapolation of trends, and relying solely on this type of analysis is not prudent. Understanding the strategy and the people employing it is of far greater value when assessing the investment risk involved.

Background Checks

Most managers will provide a list of professional and client references when asked. Of course, investment managers will provide only the names of references who will speak positively of them. Reference checks can be helpful, but often it is necessary to go further. It may be more valuable to tap into a network of information resources that includes other investment managers, consultants, brokers, bankers, auditors, attorneys, and investors. Another helpful tool can be the selective use of professional private investigators. Wall Street investigators can search for criminal or civil complaints and financial or personal problems that could interfere with the best interests of the investors.

Interviews

Manager interviews are an essential part of the evaluation process. By devoting the necessary resources (time and money) to visit managers on-site, one can identify problems and opportunities early and act decisively.

ONGOING MONITORING

Once some investors decide to hire a manager, they pay little attention to ongoing due diligence. Simply tracking the manager's performance is not sufficient. One should not underestimate the importance of maintaining regular contact with the managers as well as their peers, competitors, service providers, brokers, and other investors. A commitment to information gathering will better position an investor to monitor managers' exposures, leverage, and diversification.

INVESTING THROUGH A FUND OF HEDGE FUNDS

Unlike traditional investments, hedge funds require a distinct due diligence process that is usually best undertaken by professionals with specific expertise in alternative investments. Because of the complexity involved, investors are increasingly availing themselves of the opportunity to make alternative investment allocations through a pooled vehicle managed by a hedge fund expert, namely a fund of hedge funds (FOHF). These portfolios of hedge funds can offer the most attractive risk-adjusted rates of return with low to zero correlation to most traditional portfolios and far less volatility. (See Figure 1.2.)

For those who do not meet the definition of an accredited investor, investing in a fund of hedge funds is currently the only way to gain access to absolute return strategies in any form. Thanks to an increas-

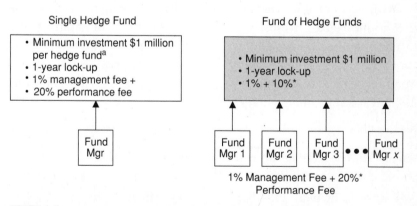

FIGURE 1.2   Two Primary Approaches to Investing in Hedge Funds.

[a]To achieve the diversification for managing risk, a substantial investor would invest in multiple hedge funds (e.g., 10, with a total investment of a minimum of $10 million in this asset class). Assuming absolute-return strategy investments comprise 10 to 30 percent of the investor's total portfolio, this approach involves investors having $35 million to $100 million in total investment assets, thereby significantly limiting the number of qualified investors having access to this investment solution.

[*]Typical performance fees range from 10%–20%.

ing number of registered FOHF, those with as little as $25,000 to invest will have more opportunities to access and benefit from absolute return investment strategies. Even individuals and institutions with substantial financial resources and significant investment experience are taking advantage of the benefits of investing completely or partially through a FOHF.

There are three main advantages of FOHF investing:

1. Professional management in the identification, evaluation, selection and monitoring process, as just outlined
2. Access to funds
3. Diversification among selected strategies and managers

In terms of access, while not true of all funds of funds, certain high-quality funds offer long-standing relationships with many of the most prominent funds in the world as well as a network of niche strategy managers. Commingled multimanager partnerships can provide access to these funds and strategies that are otherwise inaccessible. In the alternative investment field, adequate diversification is essential. Due to the volatile nature of many individual funds, investors need diversification among strategies as well as among managers within each strategy. The issue of diversification is a natural adjunct to that of access.

With account minimums at top-tier funds averaging over $1 million, an individual investor would need to make a commitment of at least $10 million to hedge funds to achieve the minimum level of diversification required. Once again, funds of funds provide the required broad diversification among strategies and managers for a significantly smaller capital commitment.

TIPS

Wealthy individuals have been investing in hedge funds since A.W. Jones & Company started the first fund in 1949. Today, thanks to the pedestrianization of hedge funds, this investment strategy is increasingly relied on by "mass affluent" investors to enhance their portfolios. How to begin, however, is often a challenge.

- Evaluate your status as an accredited investor and work with your advisor to determine the appropriate portfolio allocation to hedge funds.
- Before jumping into the asset class, learn everything you can. There is a myriad of styles and strategies, and one size does not fit all.
- Investigate the various hedge fund strategies and talk to your advisor before making a decision how to invest in hedge funds.
- Acknowledge that the concept of hedging implies a reduction of risk. If your financial advisor or others tell you hedge funds are risky, realize that this is an all-too-common assumption.
- Decide if you would be better off with a tailored hedge fund portfolio or an initial investment in a fund of hedge funds.
- Pay close attention to the fees and other investment terms of the hedge fund manager(s).
- Inquire whether managers have their own capital invested in the fund, which shows commitment and aligned interests.
- Realize that hedge fund managers seek absolute returns, not returns that are relative to the broad market. Most of the returns from hedge funds result from the managers' skills rather than the returns of an asset class. Stop thinking just of the Dow or S&P 500.
- Ask about the level of transparency and disclosure that will be provided by hedge fund managers—that is, how much information will be provided about fund activities.
- Insist on thorough, expert due diligence on hedge fund managers before entrusting them with your money.
- Remember, hedge fund investments have different tax reporting and implications from other investments. Check with your accountant before making an investment.

CHAPTER 2

Cutting through the Black Box: Transparency and Disclosure

Perhaps the biggest challenge facing the hedge fund industry as it enters into a phase of increasing maturity are the issues of transparency and disclosure. Long known for its culture of secretiveness, the hedge fund industry has begun to take a more proactive approach to balancing the need to keep investors informed while at the same time protecting the confidentiality often essential to implementing their investment strategies.

The literal meaning of the word "transparency" is the state of being easily detected or seen through, readily understood, or free from pretense or deceit. (See Figure 2.1.) But transparency of a different variety has become a central theme of discussions concerning hedge funds. Transparency in this sense refers to the ability of the investor to look through a hedge fund to its investment portfolio to determine compliance with the fund's investment guidelines and risk parameters. Transparency essentially allows investors to see what managers are doing with their money.

At first glance, the request for transparency seems like a reasonable one. After all, investors certainly would not blindly trust hedge fund managers who are managing a sizable portion of their wealth. Undoubtedly they would want to monitor not only the managers' overall performance, but also the nature of the trading activity and the risks undertaken. In comparison, the Securities and Exchange Commission

Transparency:

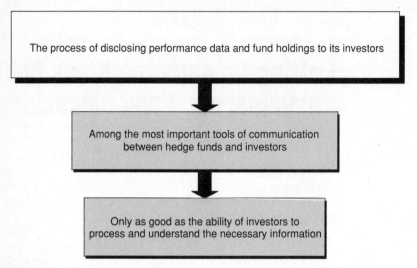

FIGURE 2.1   Transparency Defined.

(SEC) requires mutual funds to offer total transparency. Why should hedge funds be exempt from disclosing valuable information to the investing public? That question is currently under discussion by investors and regulators. Pressure of impending regulation has led to broader disclosure practices by hedge funds in recent years. (See Table 2.1.)

The quiet interworkings of a competitive capital market are another reason for increased attention to the transparency issue. Competitive pressures provide an incentive to disclose information voluntarily. As the industry matures, more investors are rejecting the historical notion that hedge funds must be accepted as black box investing that keeps them in the dark. Instead, smart investors now know that they need to look behind the curtain and that they have the right to expect sophisticated strategies to be delivered clearly and concisely. Straight talk is essential.

Fund managers not willing to disclose are facing increasing penalties in the form of difficulties in their ability to retain existing investors

TABLE 2.1   Drivers of Increased Demand for More Transparency

- Increased allocations from institutional investors (i.e. pensions, foundations)
- Governance concerns and lack of trust
- Increased regulatory attention
- Arguments from mutual funds that lack of disclosure from hedge funds undermines competitive advantage of mutual funds
- Movement toward indexing or standardization

and to attract additional investments from hedge funds, institutional investors, and more sophisticated high-net-worth individuals. As a matter of fact, often many funds of hedge funds (FDHFs) and institutional investors require managers to agree to meet minimum transparency standards prior to investing in the funds. (See Figure 2.2.)

Nevertheless, the threat of impending regulation is a real concern, and the recent heightened attention being paid to the industry is not likely to go away any time soon. This is simply a function of the industry's size and continuing rapid growth rate, the consequent involvement of more and more retail investors (ostensibly in need of some greater degree of protection than their high-net-worth or institutional counterparts), and the disproportionate influence of hedge fund activities (on the part of individual hedge funds or in various aggregates) on the overall workings of the global financial system. This latter observation

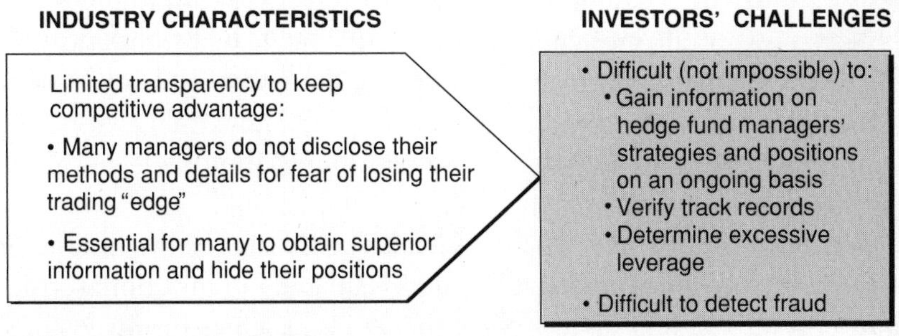

INDUSTRY CHARACTERISTICS

Limited transparency to keep competitive advantage:

- Many managers do not disclose their methods and details for fear of losing their trading "edge"

- Essential for many to obtain superior information and hide their positions

INVESTORS' CHALLENGES

- Difficult (not impossible) to:
  - Gain information on hedge fund managers' strategies and positions on an ongoing basis
  - Verify track records
  - Determine excessive leverage
- Difficult to detect fraud

FIGURE 2.2   Balance of Demands and Capabilities.

is the principal lesson learned from the Long Term Capital Management (LTCM) debacle of 1998, a lesson underscored by several subsequent smaller-scale blow-ups, where even otherwise highly sophisticated investors (i.e., two preeminent global investment banks) suffered significant losses because of inadequate oversight of their own investment in a hedge fund.

REQUEST FOR PROPOSAL PROCESS

One proponent of increased hedge fund transparency recommends that managers provide prospective investors with a completed request for proposal (RFP) document. An RFP is a written document that is part of an evaluation process (often called by the same name) used by institutional investors. This process can be summarized in the following way. (See Figure 2.3.)

Once investors determine what portion of their assets to allocate to a certain type of investment process, then they either publicly or privately solicit RFPs from appropriate managers. Those managers respond to this solicitation initially by completing a written RFP (often provided by the investor) by a certain date. The investor reviews and evaluates the submitted RFPs, selects those managers he or she considers to be best able to meet its mandate, and interviews them. This interviewing process results in a short list of managers who are invited to make a final presentation. Usually one manager is selected for the allocation.

Institutional investors use RFPs in manager searches because these documents, due diligence questionnaires or requests for information, provide information on all aspects of a firm's organization and infrastructure and the investment strategy in question. RFPs also provide these investors with a tool for comparing managers and investment strategies.

At a minimum, an RFP should address four main topics.

1. *A corporate overview.* The document should clarify the genesis of the firm, its overall objectives, and its legal and organizational structure. It also should discuss personnel issues, such as turnover, compensation, and hiring and training strategies. In addition, it should describe in detail the firm's product line and the characteristics of

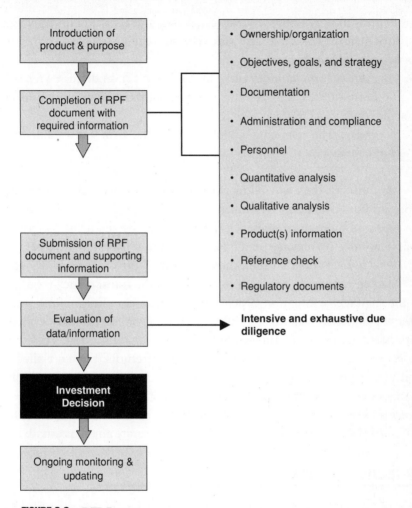

FIGURE 2.3 RFP Process.

the fund in question; it should present a chronology of the asset under management and related account information. Finally, it should disclose any legal and compliance issues the firm has been involved in and provide appropriate references.

2. *Investment strategy.* The document should explain the underlying investment process (origin and evolution, sources of return, and value-added) and implementation issues (markets traded, portfolio

composition, trading procedures). It should also explain how the firm measures and manages risk. The strategy's performance should be included in this section.

3. *Operational and administrative issues.* This section discusses reporting procedures, net asset value calculation, technology, and disaster recovery.

4. *Summary.* The summary should specify the firm's distinguishing characteristics.

This information will allow investors to accurately determine the type and kind of market risk inherent in the strategy and, correlatively, the type and amount of manager risk presented by the firm. To ensure confidentiality, managers could consider asking prospective investors to sign legal agreements that bind them to hold all information in private.

Managers must be prepared to perpetuate the transparency required in the manager evaluation process in the manager-client relationship after the allocation. Investors will require that managers provide them with open, accurate, and timely reporting and communication. They will expect to receive information on the source of returns, the asset allocation of the portfolio, portfolio composition, investment view, and any changes that have occurred at the firm or in the investment process. Reticence and secrecy after an allocation may well result in a prompt reevaluation of the manager, with the redemption of assets a real alternative.

THE TRANSPARENCY DEBATE

Two additional considerations are worth exploring before moving on to the advantages and disadvantages of hedge fund transparency from both the investor and hedge fund managers' perspectives. (See Table 2.2.)

Disclosure and Transparency: Not the Same Thing

It is important to be aware of the somewhat subtle distinction between transparency and disclosure. Hedge fund managers expect investors to go through a due diligence process, complete an RFP and are typically writing to provide a private placement memorandum (PPM) with basic written information on the fund, including an overview of investment

TABLE 2.2 Perception versus Reality in Hedge Funds

Myth: A lack of transparency is bad.

- Many hedge funds take advantage of pricing inefficiencies in securities, making a profit once prices realign as anticipated.
- Hedge funds continually seek diamonds in the rough, placing a manager at a competitive disadvantage if their positions were known.
- Competitors could replicate proprietary trading models if full transparency was provided.
- Short positions require more sensitive treatment than long positions.

strategies and operational procedures. Additionally, personal meetings provide the investor with opportunities to obtain information required to evaluate the fund.

However, the word "transparency" signifies something greater than the sum of any and all disclosures. A fund cannot provide transparency without disclosure. However, even if it discloses all its positions, what a manager is up to may not be transparent, at least to most investment professionals. For example, if a fixed-income arbitrage fund specializing in mortgage-backed securities were to provide its investors with detailed information on such arcane matters as interest only (IO) and principal only (PO) tranches, floaters and inverse floaters, and so on, such information would tell most of its investors very little about the fund's level of risk. As a matter of fact, such extensive disclosure may provide investors with a false sense of security. The required analytical skills and quantitative tools needed to analyze risk in certain strategies and instruments used by many hedge funds are costly to acquire and may not be worth the cost, given the size of one's individual investments in a hedge fund. For those investors with limited ability and cost concerns, the disclosure of key portfolio characteristics suitably aggregated may be more revealing and therefore more useful in making timely assessments of a fund risk/return profile.

Opportunity and Motive

It is necessary to keep in mind the ways in which a hedge fund's structural elements (performance fees, highly flexible investment parameters, complex, illiquid investment positions) can provide both scope and

incentive to unscrupulous (or, more critically, otherwise highly scrupu-
lous) managers to behave opportunistically to the detriment of investors
if no one is looking over their shoulders. Unless investors are investing
through FOHF, no free ride on the due diligence and monitoring is available. With no comprehensive regulatory oversight in place, investors may
feel, with some justification, that hedge fund managers have both the
motive and the opportunity to defraud them. Consequently, to protect
their interests, investors need to know what managers are up to through
increased disclosure.

Advantages and Disadvantages

With those considerations in mind, let us consider at a general level the
advantages and disadvantages of transparency from the perspective of
both the investor and hedge fund manager.

From the standpoint of hedge fund investors, more transparency
means more information available to both current and prospective investors. It means an improved ability to monitor performance and assess risks,
therefore enabling fully informed investment decision making. At the very
least, transparency enables investors to become more aware before they
commit themselves to an investment. Alternatively, it also enables them to
be more comfortable about their personal wealth invested in a fund by
reducing the levels and the likelihood of fraud, misrepresentation, and
price manipulation. Transparency also can allow investors to minimize
exposures to certain investments made by a hedge fund manager. For example, if an investor notices that the manager has a huge position in a particular security, that investor can hedge that risk by taking an opposite
position or entering into a simple derivatives contract such as an option.

From a fund manager's viewpoint, increased transparency has advantages as well. The process of disclosing data to fund investors can be
an important communication tool for the manager at the same time it
benefits investors. Managers can use disclosure to educate and maintain
dialogue with their investors, thereby keeping up relations with investors who are the long-term foundation of the hedge fund.

The overriding disadvantage of transparency from the fund manager's perspective concerns disclosure of fund holdings. The greatest
fear of fund managers is that their positions might become known to

other traders, putting them at a competitive disadvantage. This can happen easily to managers who have entered into a sizable but relatively illiquid position. For example, if a large hedge fund invested more than $500 million in a given security that was thinly traded, and the market maker in this security knew of this position, the market maker could easily work against the manager. In addition, most hedge funds seek out stocks that are not covered by mainstream analysts. They hope to find a diamond in the rough and build a large position in the stock. When managers are building such a position, it is certainly not to their advantage to have total transparency and have the fact known. These situations have resulted in disastrous trades for hedge fund managers.

Hedge fund managers also are concerned that competitors will replicate their proprietary trading models if full transparency is provided. Many managers develop highly complex, automated systems that are responsible for daily trading activity. The typical system contains an algorithm or neural net that generates signals on whether to buy or sell a given security or commodity. Traders often develop these systems after conducting intensive research on historical price trends, volatility, and other technical relationships. If competitors have access to the trades that a manager makes, they may be able to reverse engineer the models being used, again putting a manager at a significant competitive disadvantage.

Finally, managers are also reluctant to disclose positions when they have a significant short position in a particular security. Companies do not look kindly on investors who short their shares. If the company that is being shorted finds out, hedge fund managers often lose communication privileges with the company. Consequently, if a manager cannot obtain information, the trade becomes much riskier.

Common approaches to transparency include full disclosure, separate accounts, summary portfolio statistics, structured products, and registered hedge funds.

Full Disclosure

At this point it is safe to say that there is no disagreement regarding the need for transparency. The real debate centers on how much of a portfolio's position details a fund should disclose to its investors, and whether the disclosure of detailed information would make manager's actions and strategies readily understood by investors or not. Disclosure of information is only as good as the ability of investors to understand it in both timely and cost-effective manners. Analytical ability and cost considerations have led to the delivery to hedge fund investors of various forms of transparency and to the emergence of third-party financial information processing services. As a result, a small but increasing number of hedge funds are willing to provide full transparency to their investors under certain conditions. From the hedge fund manager's perspective, the bottom-line consideration to taking this approach is that where there are costs involved in preparing and releasing information and where certain types of disclosure may reveal proprietary information, transparency must be managed.

However, investors anticipating the receipt of such disclosure must grapple with a number of issues:

■ Should they purchase off-the-shelf information processing/risk management systems, if available, or should they build their own proprietary systems? Such decisions must take into consideration the complexity and variety of individual hedge fund positions, the proprietary view of risk, the level and types of risk analytics required, reporting flexibility, development costs versus licensing fees, and so on.

■ Should the project be outsourced or carried out in-house? Additional issues regarding how much to outsource, security, turnaround time, hardware, software, product support cost, and the like also need to be addressed.

Few investors are in a position to go this route alone. Existing platforms, such as RiskMetrics and Measurisk, have emerged in recent years to offer a turnkey solution to investors who require full transparency. These third-party service companies stand between a hedge fund manager willing to provide position details and investors willing to pay. These companies receive full detailed positions monthly, weekly, or daily, depending on the manager, which they then proceed to process using proprietary risk analytics before making summary reports available to paying investors. To encourage managers to provide full position reports, such companies generally also provide managers with a more condensed risk report.

The workhorse of these systems is the concept of value at risk (VaR), a measure of market risk. This measure provides an estimate of the loss that would occur with a given probability over a certain horizon. This new standard of risk measure has become very popular with financial consultants, investment board members, and many other members of the investment community, including academics. Statistically derived, it appears "objective." It is also intuitively appealing and very convenient for aggregating portfolios. However, it does not come without serious limitations. For example, it reflects everyday market behavior only; it gives no information on the direction of exposure; and it provides no information on the potential magnitude of losses in the tail of the distribution of returns.

Although the usefulness of these VaR-based systems is limited, their marketing appeal is undeniable, a fact that has not escaped the attention of many FOHFs. However, because of the high subscription cost to these risk systems and the reluctance of many managers to provide complete position details, full transparency through third-party risk platforms has been the route chosen by only a limited number of funds of hedge funds. The same cost considerations also make such a direct approach unappealing to high-net-worth investors.

Separate Accounts

Increasingly popular vehicles, separate accounts allow full disclosure to investors. Unlike investors in the main partnership, investors in a separate account own the portfolio directly and therefore have complete transparency into each position taken by the account directly from the prime brokers. Separate accounts offer additional benefits:

- Portfolio directives such as loss or exposure limits can be customized, and unwanted asset classes can be eliminated easily.
- Leverage, credit, and valuation errors or fraud can be monitored easily as can deviations from investment guidelines or style drift.

- Stop-loss rules for both individual holdings in the account and for the overall account itself also can be customized. Indeed, since investors have direct ownership, they can terminate a manager at any time and assume control of the assets.
- Further, risk analytics can be obtained directly from the prime broker at no additional charge to investors.

The extra level of transparency and control offered by separate accounts must be balanced by these facts:

- All costs incurred to manage the separate account (accounting, auditing, trading, etc.) are borne by the single investor rather than being proportionately borne by multiple investors. As a result, separate accounts bear an increased fee burden.
- Fund managers typically require a minimum of $15 million to $20 million or more to initiate a separate account. Because many hedge fund managers are unwilling to accept managed accounts, an investor insisting on this investment vehicle may have to settle for second-best managers.

Because of the large required minimums, managed accounts have been a favored investment vehicle of large investment houses, institutional investors, and a few large funds of hedge funds. But as the Beacon Hill blow-up shows, even investors of the caliber of Lehman Brothers and Société Générale with cutting-edge analytics and with the benefit of full transparency offered by separate accounts may not always be able to stop a ruthless and opportunistic manager dead in his tracks. Those who are intent on illegal or unethical activities may be difficult to detect. In Beacon Hill's case, for example, the fund's mispricing activities were caught too late.

A weakness of both separate accounts and the full disclosure through third-party systems is that neither really achieves the goal of transparency. That is to say, they still do little to keep investors appropriately informed and aware of a manager's strategies and intentions. Consider, for example, a distressed securities portfolio. A routine VaR analysis of the senior notes held in the portfolio is likely to prove meaningless. Admittedly, full disclosure of the securities in the portfolio and their prices may help investors determine that a manager is not pricing his or her own securities, that prices are consistent with prime brokers' evaluations. However, it will not shed any light on a manager's strategy and intentions. For example, the manager may be holding some corporate notes reported to be in default because he or she is anticipating a positive announcement in the short run that will increase their value. Managers may hold other notes for longer periods, waiting for the firm to come out of bankruptcy proceedings and receiving shares of equity before selling. Many other complex calculations may be involved. Unless managers directly communicate their views and horizon for each security held, transparency is unlikely to be achieved even with the best analytical tools.

Summary Portfolio Statistics

An alternative approach that has garnered wide industry support is for fund managers to disclose portfolio summary statistics instead of detailed security positions. Investors can use these statistics in tandem with other reports to monitor the overall exposure and risk of the entire portfolio. The information provided should be sufficient to clearly determine concentration levels, long and short exposure levels, leverage usage and levels of liquidity. This approach has the advantages of being cost effective, of being within the analytical reach of many investors, and of allowing for a timely assessment of a portfolio. It also provides quantitative and qualitative information without exposing proprietary trading information about the fund. A large number of managers already are providing such statistics on a monthly basis. Managers routinely provide aggregated positions by geography, sector, industry, ratings, and so on, as well as disclose their top 5 or 10 long and short positions. The goal of transparency would be further enhanced were more fund managers to provide substantive comments on their strategies and intentions relative to their aggregated sector or industry holdings while being more specific as to the rationale behind their top holdings. Such analyses will not only contribute to the education of investors but also will allay fears and suspicions by giving investors an understanding of what their hedge fund managers are up to.

Structured Products

Improved transparency also is being driven by the recent movement toward "structured" products, providing either more regulatory oversight or greater built-in transparency. These products might prove to be a bridge from current hedge funds products that provide transparency on a not-so-consistent basis to a platform of new, hybrid alternative products built to meet the increasing demands for "safer," more transparent and regulated products. (See Tables 2.3 and 2.4.)

At present there are two principal types of structured product: principal protected notes and private placement variable life insurance products.

Principal protected notes come in a variety of forms, but the traditional approach is the "zero structure" where a portion of the investor's money is invested in zero-coupon bonds guaranteeing repayment of the principal at maturity. The remaining portion is invested in a FOHF for upside potential either directly or through warrants with required liquidation of the fund of funds assets and immediate reinvestment into the risk-free asset should net asset value triggers be exceeded. Depending on the structure of the notes, exposure to the risky hedge fund portion also could be managed dynamically, leveraging and deleveraging depending on performance. More recent structures have involved insurers or banks paying for participation in the fund upside with the insurance product being structured as a two-tranche senior/junior deal.

Private placement variable life insurance products, also referred to as insurance wraps, are a portfolio of hedge funds "wrapped" inside an insurance policy. The large majority of hedge funds, which are limited

---

TABLE 2.3 Benefits of Hedge Fund-Structured Products

- Enhance returns by adding leverage
- Reduce and transforms risk:
  - □ Capture downside risk
  - □ Add new risk features
- Provide for highly customized risk exposures repackaged into new security products that provide increased accessibility that might otherwise be prohibited

TABLE 2.4 Demands for Hedge Fund–Structured Products.

Principal protection Securitizations Levered products Variable life/annuity Fund-linked notes	■ Have been available since the 1980s but now more closely associated with hedge funds and fund of hedge funds products. ■ Extremely popular in Europe already; sold through a capital-guarantee structured product. ■ Insurance groups, pension funds, and private banks are the biggest users of these products. ■ Principal guaranteed products are the most widely used products.

partnerships as opposed to limited liability companies (LLCs), are considered from a tax standpoint pass-through entities, meaning that all investment income is currently taxable. As a matter of fact, investors may be subject to a current income tax liability even though the fund may not make any cash distribution of earnings. Insurance wraps can circumvent these problems by taking advantage of a section of the Internal Revenue Code that allows investments to accumulate tax-free provided that they are within a life insurance policy. Insurance wraps offer many additional benefits that do not concern us here. An important feature of insurance wraps is that policy investments must be held in segregated accounts. They require a structure that will qualify for "look-through" treatment under the diversification rules of Treasury Reg. 1.817(h) and avoid "investor control." That is, the policyholder under an insurance wrap may not pick and choose the underlying funds on an ongoing basis. Either to satisfy providers of these principal guarantees and to manage and monitor these structures effectively or to ensure that the insurance policy can meet its policy obligations, such as death benefit payout, surrenders, and loans, hedge funds that participate in these structured products generally are held to higher standards of transparency with respect to pricing, risk management, and reporting. Attractive liquidity terms also are required. The possibility of being "stopped out" and having to liquidate does not permit investment in funds with long lock-up and redemption periods and other inflexible terms.

Registered Hedge Funds

Finally, registered hedge funds are closed-end funds that allocate money to a variety of underlying hedge funds and are registered with the SEC under the Investment Company Act of 1940 (the 1940 Act). (See Figure 2.4.) Registration with the SEC allows a fund to exceed 100 investors and avoid limitations on commodity investments, hot issues, and the number of Employee Retirement Income Security Act (ERISA) clients that pose significant compliance issues for traditional unregistered hedge funds. Funds now can attract less affluent investors by offering lower minimums. They also may become more marketable to pension funds and other institutional investors as they are no longer subject to the restrictions of ERISA, which limits the amount of money that unregistered funds can attract from retirement plans to 25 percent of total assets. However, with these benefits comes increased regulatory oversight. The SEC has successfully sought and imposed significant fines on and sanctions against advisors and their personnel and independent directors or trustees of investment companies under the 1940 Act. With independent directors being considered the "watchdog of shareholders" under the SEC regulatory oversight, the pressure to play a strong role in corporate governance and compliance is likely to translate into more stringent requirements on transparency and monitoring for both the fund and the underlying hedge funds as they meet their fiduciary responsibilities. As registered funds and structured products grow in popularity and funds vie for these sources of capital, competitive pressures are expected to bring more and more individual funds into voluntary compliance and disclosure.

REGULATORY OUTLOOK

Significant changes to the regulatory landscape relating to hedge fund disclosure requirements and practices have occurred in the last few years.

Passed to combat terrorism and money laundering through a higher degree of regulation throughout the financial industry as a result of the 9/11 terrorist attacks, the USA Patriot Act of 2001 expanded the authority of the secretary of the treasury to regulate the activities of U.S.

3C-1 FUND

Structure:

limited partnership

Exempt from SEC registration

Accredited investors

99-investor maximum

$5 to $10 million minimum

→

3C-7 FUND

Structure:

limited partnership

Exempt from SEC Registration

Qualified purchasers

499-investor maximum

$1 million minimum

→

REGISTERED, CLOSED-END FUND

1940 Act and/or 1933 Act

registered fund

SEC-registered product

Accredited investors

Unlimited investors

Minimums as low as $25,000

FIGURE 2.4 What Is a Registered Hedge Fund?

financial institutions, particularly relations with foreign individuals and entities. The Sarbanes-Oxley Act, also passed in the wake of recent corporate scandals, has added more weapons to the regulators' arsenal when they weigh in on issues such as disclosure and auditing standards and ethics.

The SEC included a discussion of hedge fund transparency in its September 2003 staff report entitled "Implications of the Growth of Hedge Funds." The report acknowledged the fact that the financial press is reporting increased interest in risk transparency and notes that this trend may be attributable to increased hedge fund investments by pensions, endowments, foundations, and other institutional investors.

On a broader note, investors increasingly need to question transparency standards as they relate to large institutional investors versus smaller investors. While standard fees and liquidity terms are typical, several areas deserve a closer look, namely special investor considerations and soft dollar practices.

As stated, hedge fund investors purchase a privately placed security, usually a limited partnership interest, in which all investors are subject to the same terms. However, large investors increasingly are offered special considerations in exchange for substantial investments. Varying reporting standards, fee concessions, liquidity terms, and other consideration often is given in exchange for large commitments. A question therefore arises: If all investors are purchasing the same security, why are some investors given preferential access to data and disclosure that could potentially give them an economic advantage over other investors? For example, if a large investor receives preferred portfolio inspection rights on a weekly basis, and most other investors receive only a quarterly investor letter, that large investor may learn of changes in the portfolio.

Soft dollars are another of the latest specters hanging over Wall Street. In the hedge fund industry, their abuses have the potential to be more suspect and egregious. As brokerage commission expenses that are typically charged to a fund on behalf of fund investors, soft dollars allow managers to use part of the commissions to pay for research expenses involved in portfolio management. Presumably, investors do not mind paying an extra couple of cents per share to strengthen the research process and resources of their investment managers. However, the scenario becomes problematic when the allocation of these expenses is abused. Remember, many asset management firms generate tens of millions of dollars of commissions from brokerage firms each year.

As hedge fund assets and regulatory oversight increase, the industry should expect a higher level of professional due diligence execution through specialized, private Wall Street trading firms. Hedge fund managers are playing Russian roulette with building their businesses around inconsistent terms, conditions, and side deals. Corporate America and the mutual fund industry have come under serious regulatory scrutiny, which will inevitably spill over into the hedge fund world. The SEC recently has requested a meaningful increase in its budget for hedge fund industry enforcement officers, and changes are likely to come sooner than later.

Investors need to insist on the level of transparency with which they are comfortable and should invest their money only with those who meet these requirements on an ongoing basis.

TIPS

As the hedge fund industry matures and caters to a broader group of investors, transparency is a popular topic of discussion. In a nutshell, transparency is the ability to see what a hedge fund manager is doing with investors' money. Although hedge funds historically have been somewhat secretive, more investors than ever are unwilling to accept hedge funds as black box investing where little is known about the fund's activities.

- Begin your evaluation of hedge fund managers with a thorough due diligence process that includes personal meetings and a review of basic written information on the fund.
- Consider issuing a request for proposal (RFP) to inquire about the firm's background, organization, and investment strategy.
- As part of your due diligence, inquire about transparency, which is not the same thing as disclosure. Ask how much the

hedge fund manager will divulge on an ongoing basis about fund positions, for example. The answer will tell you the level of transparency provided by the manager. The right amount of information varies by hedge fund strategy.

■ Ask whether the hedge fund manager provides full disclosure. An increasing number of hedge funds are willing to provide full transparency to their investors under guarded, well-managed conditions.

■ Look into creation of a separate account, which also provides full disclosure, yet requires that an investor own the portfolio directly, unlike an investor in the main partnership. While more burdensome from an administrative perspective, this approach has merit.

■ If full disclosure is not offered, inquire about availability of portfolio summary statistics. Some fund managers who are unwilling to disclose detailed security positions will agree to this lower level of transparency, which represents an alternative approach that has garnered wide industry support.

■ Consider one of the new structured products, such as a principal protected note or insurance wrapper, which are built to meet the increasing demands for "safer," more transparent and regulated products.

■ Evaluate whether an investment in a registered hedge fund is right for you. These closed-end funds allocate money to a variety of underlying hedge funds and are registered with the Securities and Exchange Commission, which provides regulatory oversight.

■ Use transparency to minimize exposures to certain investments made by the hedge fund manager. For example, if a manager has a large position in a particular security, you may choose to hedge that risk either by taking an opposite position or by entering into a simple derivatives contract such as an option.

■ Keep abreast of news coverage of hedge fund regulatory issues, which is a reflection of the pressure regarding hedge fund disclosure standards.

CHAPTER 3

The Operational Risk Crisis

As the hedge fund industry has grown explosively, so too has the list of fund failures and burned investors, many of whom did not have advance knowledge of potential warning signs. It seems as if we are constantly faced with news reports about catastrophic losses incurred by some of the industry's best-known managers, and even those investors who insist on a comprehensive due diligence process are not immune. To better understand why hedge funds fail and how these failures could be avoided, Capco conducted a recent study to assess why failures occur in the hedge fund industry.

The findings of the study are compelling. The main area of concern is that operational issues account for 50 percent of hedge fund failures, an alarmingly high percentage. With that in mind, the key point of interest to hedge fund investors is that they must expand their due diligence and monitoring practices to ensure that they understand the back-office capabilities of the hedge funds with which they are contemplating an investment. This understanding can make a big difference in preventing or avoiding a bad investment decision.

As background, it should be noted that this study is based on a database of hedge fund failures that dates back 20 years and captures details of losses, litigation, and root causes. Failed funds are considered those that had been forced to cease investment operations suddenly and where investors faced a significant or total loss of capital. This differs from a

*Stuart Feffer, PhD, and Christopher Kundro

more common discretionary fund closure, where a manager chooses to unwind a fund over time and in an orderly manner. The findings are based on over 100 failed funds over this period. The primary cause of each fund's failure attributed to at least one of these factors representing three basic categories of risk:

1. *Investment Risk.* These risks are market and related risks associated with the investment style of the fund or the securities it held.
2. *Business Risk.* These risks are associated with the management of the fund company as a business that are not directly related to market movements, such as failure to reach a base level of assets under management or a change in management of the fund.
3. *Operational Risk.* These risks are associated with supporting the operating environment of the fund. The operating environment includes middle- and back-office functions such as trade processing, accounting, administration, valuation, and reporting.

Investment risk is the type of risk that fund investors generally intend to take in exchange for the promise of performance. Business risk includes factors that stem from the possibility that the fund manager simply will be unable to create a sustainable business. Operational risks are all of the other types of risks that investors do not intend to take as part of their investment strategy, namely the risk that an investment might be fraudulent, that the infrastructure might fail, or that managers might misrepresent performance.

In circumstances where it is difficult to isolate the leading causes of a fund's failure to a single category, failure is attributable to a combination of multiple risks that span these categories.

To understand common operational due diligence practices employed in the industry, informal interviews and discussions with hedge fund managers and consultants were conducted. The conclusion is that an alarmingly high proportion of hedge fund failures can be attributed to operational issues. Indeed, 54 percent of failed funds had identifiable operational issues and half of all failures could be attributed to operational risk alone.

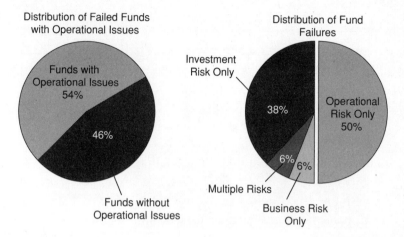

FIGURE 3.1   Operational Issues and Primary Causes of Fund Failure.

The most common operational issues related to hedge fund losses have been misrepresentation of fund investments, misappropriation of investor funds, unauthorized trading, and inadequate resources. (See Figure 3.1.)

Misrepresentation of investments is defined as the act of creating or causing the generation of reports and valuations with false and misleading information. This may be due to deliberate deception (e.g., to hide poor investment performance) or to operational errors.

Misappropriation of funds/general fraud includes managers who knowingly move money or assets out of the fund either for personal use or as an outright theft. Unauthorized trading and style breaches cover fund managers who make investments outside of the stated fund strategy or change the fund's investment style without investor approval. This is also known as unmonitored style drift and is included as an operational risk factor because it exposes investors to unintended risks that occasionally result in fund failure.

Inadequate resources for fund strategy(s) is problematic when technology, processes, or personnel are not able to properly handle operating volumes or the types of investments and activities in which the fund engages. (See Figure 3.2.)

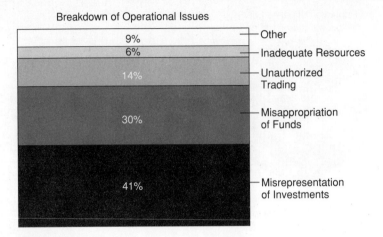

FIGURE 3.2   Distribution of Operational Issues Contributing to Operational Risk in Hedge Funds.

These problems contributed to substantial investor losses in hedge funds that might have been prevented or avoided with a more comprehensive investor due diligence and monitoring approach. For example, in the case of the recent failure of the Lipper convertible arbitrage funds, we believe that had investors scrutinized and monitored the funds' valuation practices closely, there is a good chance that they would have recognized the absence of separation of duties in the pricing of illiquid securities and either avoided investing in these funds or insisted on changes that might have prevented the problem.

Of funds that failed as the result of operational risk only, nearly half had multiple operational issues. (See the sample cases in Table 3.1.)

The most frequent combination of operational issues was misappropriation of investor funds and misrepresentation of fund investments. (See Figure 3.3.)

Misrepresentation of fund investments and activities is clearly a major problem as seen by its prevalence among failed funds and its relationship to other issues and risks. Although most managers do not set out to defraud investors from day 1, many clearly have done so. We have found numerous occasions where on the back of poor investment performance, managers "modified" the valuation of their funds and/or their

TABLE 3.1 Sample Cases

Strategy: Market Neutral **Total Estimated Loss/Redemption:** $700+ Million **Primary Operational Issue:** Unauthorized Trading **Highlights:** ■ Fund marketed as a market-neutral fund. ■ Betting on drop in interest rates leveraged 10 to 1. ■ Lost 60% of value in 7 months.	**Strategy:** Fixed Income Arbitrage **Total Estimated Loss/Redemption:** $500+ Million **Primary Operational Issue:** Inadequate Resources/ Infrastructure **Highlights:** ■ Fund had a steady track record for many years. ■ Shifted to new trading/investment strategy. ■ Risk management system could not fully support new security types. ■ Resulted in high volatility leading to losses and drawdowns.
Strategy: Convertible Arbitrage and International **Total Estimted Loss:** $300+ Million **Primary Operational Issue:** Misrepresentation of Investments **Highlights:** ■ Hedge fund manager wrote down $315 million. ■ Attributed it to a conservative pricing of illiquid securities. ■ Pricing was done without third-party verification.	**Strategy:** Long/Short Equity **Total Estimated Loss:** $40+ Million **Primary Operational Issue:** Misappropriation of Funds/Fraud **Highlights:** ■ Funds had initial minimal loss that was hidden. ■ Funds manager misrepresented performance. ■ Attracted additional investments and opened more funds. ■ Management used fund assets for personal expenses.

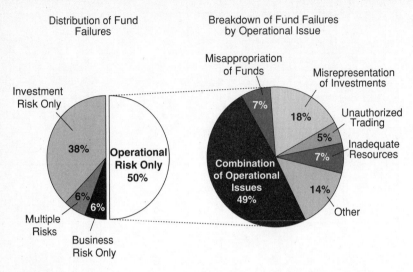

Distribution of Fund Failures

Breakdown of Fund Failures by Operational Issue

FIGURE 3.3   Breakdown of Fund Failures Attributed to Operational Risk Only by Operational Issue.

investment results to buy time until actual results improved. In some cases, when results did not improve, the modifications often became more and more aggressive, were eventually discovered, and required a write-down of assets. In these cases, the sudden correction usually led to a total collapse of the fund.

Although it may be impossible to foresee which managers will attempt to defraud investors, it is critical that investors understand the extent to which the opportunity exists to manipulate and misrepresent fund investments, should managers feel the urge. Investors can determine this information through more complete scrutiny of a hedge fund's operations and technology capabilities and a detailed understanding of the information flows between a fund and its supporting service providers, which typically include prime brokers and administrators. Knowing that a fund has in place tight controls over cash flows and seeks third-party verification of a valuation to insure that it is current and appropriate will not eliminate the risk of fraud, but it will go a long way in limiting the manager's opportunity to perpetrate fraud.

Relying solely on a fund's administrators and auditors may not be enough, however. For example, to hide substantial investment losses, the Manhattan Fund allegedly created fictitious account statements that materially overstated the value of the fund. These statements were provided to investors, potential investors, as well as the fund's administrator and auditor for more than three years with neither the administrator nor the auditor catching the problem. As Figure 3.4 shows, misrepresentation is a critical issue.

OPERATIONAL DUE DILIGENCE: AN IMPORTANT PART OF THE INVESTMENT PROCESS

Operational due diligence is an important part of the investment process. Although it can help address some fundamental questions affecting investment decisions, it tends to be the least monitored of all risks related to hedge funds. Properly executed, operational due diligence is a complement to the normal investment due diligence that institutional investors and professional advisors undertake for their clients before recommending a fund for investment. This investment due diligence typically includes background checks on all of the principal parties in the fund management company as well as investigations of investment style, past performance, trading practices, and other aspects of the investment process. The supplemental operational due diligence that we suggest, however, also focuses on:

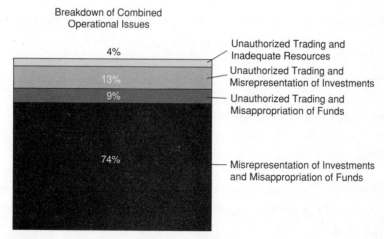

FIGURE 3.4 Breakdown of Most Frequent Combinations of Operational Issues.

- Transparency of underlying positions in the invested funds for use in generating risk analysis and tracking potential style drift
- Capacity, or selecting funds that have capacity to accept additional subscriptions
- Survivorship, or confidence that the underlying funds will continue to operate to alleviate the need for reallocation of invested funds
- Flow of funds to ensure the proper controls, processes, and information links are in place to allow quick valuations and timely allocation and investment of subscriptions

TRADITIONAL APPROACHES TO OPERATIONAL REVIEWS

Investors should add operational risk questions to their standard due diligence request for information. Questions might include:

- Is there an ancillary component of the overall investment due diligence process?
- Is asset allocation based on a generic view across multiple managers, fund types, and strategies?
- Is the fund's team focused on specific functions?
- Is the fund focused on specific aspects of the operating environment?
- Is due diligence specifically focused internally on the organizational structure?
- Is qualitative due diligence only often reduced to a background check and character assessment of fund managers?

Information about the efficiency, effectiveness, capacity, and control of hedge funds is rarely assessed in sufficient detail to inform investment decisions and identify appropriate mitigation opportunities. With that in mind, here are five key characteristics of an effective operational due diligence approach for hedge funds:

1. It provides a comprehensive view of the structure, quality, and control of the people, operations, technology, and data supporting the fund.

2. It covers internal processes, systems, and information flows.
3. It covers the processes, systems, information flows, and interfaces provided by external parties such as prime brokers, administrators, custodians, and so on.
4. It analyzes the unique requirements of each fund/strategy as they can vary considerably depending on fund objectives and investment style.
5. Assessments are updated on a periodic and event-driven basis.

The hedge fund industry only gets more challenging from here. Every indication is that it is expected to maintain its steep growth trajectory. Investors should expect that the anticipated growth in hedge fund investing will be accompanied by increased performance and operational demands as the number of new managers grows, the breadth and complexity of investment strategies expands, and new forms of regulation are considered and eventually adopted.

All of this suggests that the operational risks associated with these investments will only grow more important. For the hedge fund investor, effective operational due diligence and monitoring will be key to reducing the potential of catastrophic losses and improving long-term investment results in this sector.

TIPS

Hedge fund blow-ups and stories of burned investors remain all too common in spite of increased discussion of expert due diligence and transparency. To examine the root causes of hedge fund failures, Capco recently studied more than 100 hedge funds and 20 years' worth of data to evaluate hedge fund losses and litigation. The study's key finding is that operational issues account for more than 50 percent of these failures, which indicates the need for careful study of a hedge fund's back office prior to making an investment.

- Before investing, be sure to understand the hedge fund's potential for investment risk (the investment style of the fund or its securities), business risk (risks related to the sustainability of the business), and operational risk (middle- and back-office functions).
- Ask the hedge fund manager about style drift (changing the fund's investment style without investor approval). When style drift is unmonitored, it may expose investors to unintended risks.
- Determine if the fund's technology and personnel are well equipped to handle the proper level of operating volumes or types of investments in which the fund engages.
- Monitor the possibility of misrepresentation of investments, which occurs when a hedge fund manager provides false or misleading information, often to hide poor investment performance or errors.
- Watch out for misappropriation of funds and fraud, which may happen if a hedge fund manager knowingly moves assets out of the fund for personal use or as theft.
- Scrutinize and monitor fund valuation practices through ongoing due diligence.
- Check on the hedge fund's underlying positions to generate risk analysis and track potential style drift.
- Evaluate survivorship and gain confidence that the underlying funds will continue to operate to alleviate the need for reallocation of invested funds.
- Be sure that the proper controls are in place to allow quick valuations and timely allocation and investment of subscriptions.

CHAPTER 4

Best Practices in
Hedge Fund Valuation

Recent news reports on hedge fund valuation problems have drawn increased attention to the issue of risk tolerance and the role it plays in an investment strategy. Valuation issues figure prominently in the Securities and Exchange Commission's recent staff report on hedge funds and in news accounts such as the high-profile departure of a top fund manager at a leading hedge fund group. They also come into play in the market-timing scandals of the mutual fund world since mutual fund valuations created the opportunity for market timers in the first place.

Hedge fund investors should heed the results of Capco's recent study on the root causes of hedge fund failures, which identified operational risk factors that together seem to account for approximately half of catastrophic cases. Red flags to watch for include misappropriation of funds and fraud; misrepresentation; unauthorized trading or trading outside of guidelines; and resource/infrastructure insufficiencies. Issues related to valuation—the determination of fair market value for all of the positions that make up a fund—underlie many of these operational risk factors.

Most of the instances of fraud and misrepresentation involved some form of deception regarding the value of assets held by the fund, and many of the resource/infrastructure problems we studied eventually man-

---

*Stuart Feffer, PhD, and Christopher Kundro

ifested themselves through some form of inability to accurately price or risk the fund's book. While valuation issues were not specifically identified in our original study as a major category of operational risk on its own, various aspects of the valuation problem have played either a primary or a contributing role in more than a third (35 percent) of cases of failures that we studied.

This information suggests that the industry is not yet taking the steps needed to address problems in the valuation process. In fact, we believe that issues related to valuation of portfolios likely will become the next major black eye for the hedge fund industry. Unless certain practices become more widespread, we believe that the hedge funds face a potential crisis of confidence with investors. Therefore, we caution investors to study the valuation of their hedge fund portfolios more closely, in particular as they pertain to the issue of managing operational risks associated with hedge fund investments.

The issue of valuations in hedge fund portfolios concerns how to ensure that a fund uses fair and proper prices for positions that it holds. The net value of these positions, after fees and expenses, is the Net Asset Value (NAV) of the fund and is used as the basis for all subscriptions, redemptions, and performance calculations.

For some types of investments, in particular for nonconcentrated positions in liquid securities, fair and impartial valuations are fairly easy to achieve. Recent transaction prices as well as marketable bids and offers are readily available and are visible on major wires and feeds, such as Bloomberg and Reuters. For many other investments favored by some types of hedge funds, this is not necessarily the case; some securities may trade infrequently, and transactional prices may not be available. In these instances, broker quotes must be sought to get a sense for what the position is worth. Some securities are highly complex and may be difficult to value without use of a mathematical model. However, in thinly traded markets quotes can be difficult to obtain and may be unreliable. Broker quotes for some types of mortgage-backed securities can easily vary by 20 to 30 percent. Mathematical models make use of assumptions and forecasts that are subjective and open to question.

Combine these natural, inherent difficulties in pricing complex or illiquid investments with a powerful financial incentive to show strong, or hide weak, performance, and then situate these factors in an environment with minimal regulatory oversight or without strict discipline and internal controls (still far too typical in the hedge fund industry), and there is potential for trouble.

Trouble is precisely what the industry has seen. At Lipper Convertible, a convertible bond hedge fund that collapsed recently, several portfolio managers apparently made use of the opacity of the convertibles market to misvalue their portfolio significantly. Similar issues were behind the collapse of Beacon Hill and other well-publicized funds.

It certainly seems that these kinds of issues are increasing in their frequency, severity, and visibility and deserve closer attention by investors. Three key trends have driven the increased incidence of valuation problems.

1. The increasing sophistication of financial instruments means that new types of structures are invented constantly. Their complexity often make them difficult to price, and it can be very difficult to guarantee standard or accurate pricing procedures. In many of these cases, valuation issues can be compounded due to the inherent or synthetic leverage of many of these instruments.
2. The increasing number of funds that are using complex instruments also causes concern. As the hedge fund market grows, new managers are emerging every day, and many are focused on parts of the market where pricing and valuation issues are most prevalent.
3. A broadening investor base has resulted as institutional investors increase their allocations to hedge funds and as some institutions that have not previously been sizable hedge fund investors aggressively enter the market. In addition, the fact that many fund of hedge funds are building hedge fund products for middle-market and affluent retail investors also increases the number of hedge fund investors. This increased attention to the sector has resulted in increasing regulatory and media scrutiny.

Because of this increased attention to the hedge funds at a time when the factors that make pricing and valuation difficult are becoming even more prevalent, we believe that valuation problems will likely continue to occur and to attract significant attention from the financial and general business press.

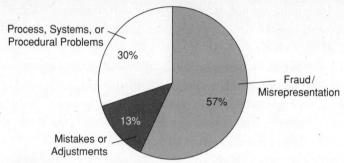

FIGURE 4.1   Causes of Valuation Issues Implicated in Hedge Fund Failures.

CAUSES OF VALUATION PROBLEMS

Valuation-related problems at a hedge fund generally are caused by fraud or misrepresentation, mistakes or adjustments, and/or procedural problems. (See Figure 4.1.)

Fraud/Misrepresentation

Occasionally a valuation problem will be part of a deliberate attempt to inflate the value of a fund, to hide unrealized losses, to be able to report stronger performance, or to cover up broader theft and fraud. This appears to have been true, for example, in the case involving the failure a few years ago of the Manhattan Fund. In 57 percent of the cases we studied, fraud misrepresentation was the cause of fund failure.

Mistakes or Adjustments

As mentioned, some securities often traded by hedge funds can be extremely difficult to value. Even when prices are readily available, some positions may require adjustment anyway. Positions that comprise a large proportion of a single issue, for example, should be discounted to reflect the likelihood that they cannot be liquidated without a significant market impact. Also, if a security is held in a large enough quantity where public disclosure (e.g., Schedule 13D) is required, an adjustment may need to be made if all or part of the position cannot be sold anonymously. Occasionally positions will simply be mismarked, and may cause a sudden and unexpected impact to fund valuation when the marks are corrected or the position is reversed. There also can be a significant variation depending on which "correct" price is being used— bid, offer, or midpoint. This is especially the case when it comes to thinly traded or illiquid instruments where bid/offer spreads can be sizable. Mistakes or adjustments were implicated in 13 percent of the fund failures we studied.

Process, Systems, or Procedural Problems

There are times when a fund may be following its own policies consistently and accurately, but a flaw in the valuation procedures or process causes a systemic mismarking of the book. This is most common in cases where a fund is trading instruments that cannot be handled by its regular processing systems, and some kind of workaround is devised that later proves to be flawed. Issues that may occur include not only incorrect pricing but complete positions being incorrectly captured on the fund's books and records. Sometimes total positions are completely excluded in error. Mortgages, bank loans, over-the-counter (OTC) derivatives, convertible bonds, and nondollar instruments of all kinds can be prone to these kinds of issues if underlying systems do not fully support them.

Sometimes, even when technology support is robust and procedures are both well defined and widely monitored, flaws in the valuation process can have wide-ranging effects. In the recent mutual fund market-timing scandals, for instance, a flaw in the basic rules around fund valuations created much of the opportunity for market timing in the first place. This situation occurred because reported values of funds as of the end of the standard market day in the United States without adjustment for news that may have moved markets.

Other procedural factors that can affect valuation include the process by which a quote is obtained from a third party, such as a broker/dealer,

as a basis for valuation. Investors should assess whether the broker/
dealer is a counterparty to the transaction and therefore has a potential conflict of interest. Is the individual who is providing the quote a
senior executive who is truly capable of providing an accurate price,
especially when complex modeling is involved? The point is that sometimes the devil is in the details, namely the task-level procedures for
obtaining prices on a regular basis. Process, procedural, or systems
problems accounted for 30 percent of these valuation-related failures in
our study.

SOUND PRACTICES FOR VALUATION

The likelihood of valuation problems occurring can be reduced and
their effects mitigated, should they occur, if the hedge fund industry
begins to adopt some sound practices that have been common in other
parts of the financial industry for some time.

Although it is possible for any fund to experience valuation issues,
in our experience some types of funds are more prone to the problem
than others, and this fact should be taken into account as part of the
investment process. Unless there is some kind of broader fraud or mal-
feasance, funds that invest exclusively in highly liquid instruments for
which prices are readily available (e.g., most U.S. and major-market
equities) are far less likely to significantly mismark a portfolio than funds
that trade complex OTC instruments or illiquid securities.

We caution fund managers and investors to take particular care in
looking at valuation procedures for these seven types of instruments:

1. Convertible bonds
2. Mortgages, mortgage-backed securities, and asset-backed securities
3. Credit-default swaps
4. Other over-the-counter derivatives
5. Bank debt and loans, distressed debt
6. Nondollar and emerging markets
7. Highly concentrated positions and positions that make up a large
   proportion of a single issue

Convertible Bonds

Convertibles can be extremely complex to value and can be limited in liquidity. Broker quotes for convertibles can vary significantly for the same issue, and it can be difficult to determine the size for which any given quote is good. In one convertible portfolio, for example, the average difference between highest and lowest bid on the same issue was around 5 percent, with the largest deltas as high as 20 percent.

Mortgages, Mortgage-Backed Securities, and Asset-Backed Securities

These funds are also difficult to value and may be subject to both liquidity problems and high dispersion of market-maker quotes. They also have special processing requirements, and most firms that trade them must use a dedicated system for booking, valuing, and processing these securities. Funds that trade these instruments as part of a broader fixed-income strategy, therefore, often are carrying mortgage and asset-backed securities on a different system from the rest of the portfolio, requiring either integration or manual intervention to consolidate. These systems and procedures should get special attention by fund management or during investor due diligence.

Credit Default Swaps

Credit derivatives are growing in popularity and often are used by hedge funds to take on credit exposure or to hedge a portfolio. Depending on the specific circumstances of the issuer covered by the swap, these also can be difficult to unwind, and market-maker quotes can be difficult to obtain.

Other Over-the-Counter Derivatives

New types of complex swaps, options, and hybrids are developed constantly, and some hedge funds make use of highly customized instruments in their portfolios. Procedures for valuing and booking these trades should receive special attention.

Bank Debt and Loans, Distressed Debt

These securities are often both illiquid and difficult to model, requiring significant credit expertise.

Nondollar and Emerging Markets

Many funds that begin with a focus on U.S. markets will put in place an infrastructure that accommodates U.S. dollar–denominated securities, but may not properly book and track nondollar securities. If these funds begin to trade in other markets without upgrading their infrastructure, this additional processing complexity can create an environment that is more prone than average to valuation mistakes and processing problems. Securities issued in some emerging markets, even when a fund is experienced with nondollar investing, can be difficult to value and may be subject to liquidity concerns as well.

Highly Concentrated Positions and Positions
That Make Up a Large Proportion of a Single Issue

As mentioned, even when in a highly liquid security that is not difficult to price, these types of positions may require adjustments to reflect the true liquidation value of the position and the fact that it cannot be disposed of without a significant market impact.

    It is worth noting that while complex, thinly traded, or illiquid instruments are more likely to have pricing issues, even fairly actively traded securities with prices readily available from independent third-party sources occasionally can be "stale" due to bad market feeds, human error, or other issues. Pricing issues have been publicly discussed as an issue with mutual funds in recent months. Investors should take steps during due diligence to ensure that all automated prices are validated prior to month-end valuations and as part of other reporting and subscription/redemption cycles.

We believe that these problems could be largely mitigated or averted if investors insist that the hedge fund industry adopt certain practices related to valuations that have long been common in other parts of the financial sector. In particular, investors should insist on strict independence and separation of duties; ensure consistency in the valuation process; and require a level of management supervision and oversight.

INSIST ON STRICT INDEPENDENCE AND SEPARATION OF DUTIES

Separation of duties and independence in mark to market has long been a fundamental principle of control in financial institutions, but is still inconsistently applied in the hedge fund industry. A breakdown in separation of duties seems to have been a factor in almost every valuation-related hedge fund failure that we have studied. In short, independence and separation of duties means that the person who performs, checks, or approves valuations should not receive incentives or inducements based directly on the performance of the investment being valued, and should not report to managers who do so.

The trader or portfolio manager should never perform final valuations, although often it makes sense for the traders or managers to do their own valuations as a "reasonableness check" on an independent process. Whenever possible an independent third party who does not work for the fund management company should check valuations prepared by the managers themselves. A fund manager should keep a financial/accounting staff independent of the portfolio management team to prepare and validate marks to market. In most cases, these staff members will report to the chief financial officer or the chief operating officer of the fund management company, and should be compensated based on the overall profitability results of the management company rather than directly based on the performance of any of the investment vehicles managed by the firm.

In some cases, fund administrators will perform this role for a fund manager. Some valuation services also will prepare marks on an "outsourced" basis for a fund manager. Many funds also employ an auditor to test valuations used for financial statements to investors. We believe that a fund manager always should use an external third party to verify that portfolio valuations are accurate before they are reported to investors. This external third party would be used in addition to the fund auditor, who often examines valuations less frequently and after they have been reported.

ENSURE CONSISTENCY IN THE VALUATION PROCESS

Daily mark to market and monthly/quarterly prestatement valuations always should be performed according to a well-defined process, and the application of sources, methods, rules, and models always should be applied consistently, with any deviations or unusual circumstances clearly noted and documentation saved.

These processes may change over time in response to changes in the markets for certain types of securities, to make use of better information, or for other good management reasons. However, when it appears that valuation choices are made situationally, without a clear, documented rationale, we believe that investors should seriously consider the safety of their capital.

REQUIRE A LEVEL OF SUPERVISION AND OVERSIGHT

If the fund managers perform valuations themselves, there should be a set of clearly documented policies and procedures, as well as a way of ensuring that those polices and procedures are actually followed in practice. Generally, this is accomplished through external validation, testing, and audit.

After the collapse of Lipper Convertibles, Ken Lipper commented to the media through his attorney that he was unaware of any mispricing issues prior to the collapse of the fund and that it had been valued by the portfolio managers responsible for handling its investments. If true, this situation represents an abdication of management's duty to oversee the valuation process. Management should review valuations; there should be evidence that pricing discrepancies have been brought to management's attention; and action should be taken when appropriate. Especially in a fund that invests in the problem-prone instruments mentioned earlier, a certain number of honest valuation discrepancies are inevitable. Whether fund managers acknowledge the occurrence of such discrepancies, how they are handled, and whether the results are documented can speak volumes about the quality of supervision over the valuation process. This management oversight is critical to ensuring the soundness and safety of investor assets in a fund.

Sometimes it can be smart for a fund manager to outsource some of the mechanics to a third-party pricing service. Even for complex instruments, such as certain OTC derivatives and asset-backed securities, service providers can price these instruments and also offer operations outsourcing and risk management services. We believe that any move which increases the independence and objectivity of the valuation process should be viewed positively by investors.

Clearly, pricing and valuation have become a significant issue for the hedge fund industry, and we believe that its significance is likely to increase—particularly as it relates to funds that trade strategies and instruments that are particularly prone to the types of problems we discuss here. But we believe that a set of practices long standard in other parts of the financial sector can mitigate losses and prevent problems, at least in many cases. These represent the hedge fund industry's best chance at avoiding a damagingly public black eye.

TIPS

Valuation issues relate to the determination of fair market value for all of the positions that make up a fund. They are a key component of operational risk and a primary reason for many hedge fund failures. Because the hedge fund industry is not doing enough to address valuation, a recent report cautioned investors to scrutinize the valuation of their hedge fund portfolios and consider how they relate to the issue of managing operational risks. Investors need to insist that the hedge fund industry adopt stricter practices related to valuation, as is already the case in other areas of the financial sector.

- Understand that it is difficult to price complex or illiquid investments, but that the potential for trouble is significant enough to require close attention to valuation issues.
- Be sure the hedge fund uses fair prices for its positions by checking the net value of these positions, after fees and expenses. This is called the Net Asset Value (NAV) of the fund, which is the basis for all subscriptions, redemptions, and performance calculations.
- Check recent transaction prices as well as marketable bids and offers on major wires and feeds, such as Bloomberg and Reuters.
- Some securities that trade infrequently may not have readily available transactional prices. Seek a broker quote to get a sense of what the position is worth.
- Highly complex securities may require development of a mathematical model, although such a model may be subjective.
- Watch for valuation problems that arise from a deliberate attempt to inflate fund value, possibly to mask unrealized losses or to cover up a theft or fraud.
- Monitor positions that may be mismarked, which results in a sudden, unexpected impact to fund valuation when the marks are corrected later or the position is reversed.
- Understand that problems may relate to procedural problems that occur when a fund follows its own policies, but when a flaw in the valuation procedures or process causes a systemic mismarking of the fund's book.
- Assess whether the fund's broker/dealer is a counterparty to the transaction and therefore has a potential conflict of interest.
- Certain types of funds are more prone to valuation problems than others, such as credit default swaps, highly concentrated positions, and convertible bonds. Take this fact into account as part of the investment process.

CHAPTER 5

Does Size Matter?

To what extent does a hedge fund's growth and size affect its prospects for maximum performance, and how does this affect its investors?

Investors need to model their investment portfolio to ensure proper diversification among strategies, yet the findings of a recent study show that investors also need to evaluate funds of all sizes when making hedge fund allocations. Although the tendency may be for investors to believe that "bigger is better" and to invest with the large, high-profile funds, that is not always the right move.

The study's implication is that small funds tend to outperform larger funds and that medium-size funds typically fare the worst. Therefore, manager selection should be biased toward those hedge funds that are nimble and responsive and that generate alpha. Smaller funds can put all of their money into their best ideas; larger, more senior funds often find it difficult to put continued inflows to work due to the constraints of internal asset allocation guidelines and policies.

The number of hedge fund managers is up from approximately 1,000 in the late 1990s to more than 6,000 in 2003, which makes it increasingly important to rely on rigorous due diligence when selecting the best-performing managers within the various investment styles and strategies. Although the number of managers has grown overall, the ratio of hedge fund start-ups to closings within the hedge fund industry generates concerns over basic issues related to back-office operations, transparency, capacity, and style drift, many of which have been discussed in

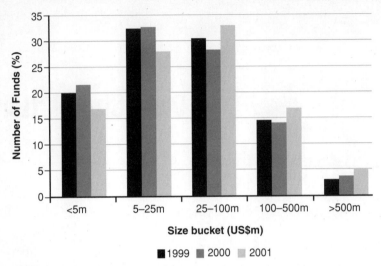

FIGURE 5.1   Size Distribution of Hedge Hunds.
Source: Van Hedge Fund Advisors.

previous chapters. While approximately 700 to 800 hedge funds closed in 2002, another 800 to 900 new firms began operations.

The question regarding the link between portfolio size and diminishing returns evolved from observations of top hedge fund managers in large funds, such as Tiger and Soros, who left to start successful hedge funds that closed to new investment at $500 million or $1 billion, which is far smaller than the funds where they began their careers. At its peak, Tiger had reached $22 billion, and Soros had reached $23 billion.

As background, consider that as a group, hedge funds are relatively smaller than their financial counterparts when measured in terms of assets, staff size, and years in business. During the three-year period between 1999 and 2001, LJH confirmed that size distribution remained fairly constant with slightly more than half of all hedge funds smaller than $25 million, approximately 80 percent of hedge funds smaller than $100 million, and 5 percent of all hedge funds larger than $500 million. (See Figure 5.1.) Although many investors do not consider investing with firms smaller than $50 million, the data support the view that these are indeed strong-performing funds.

According to the 2002 Putnam-Lovell paper on the possible institutionalization of hedge funds, statistical observation suggests that the distribution of hedge funds by size continues to trend downward slightly. The average hedge fund size is $87 million with a median base of $22 million. The implications of this might be an increase in niche opportunities and new strategies, as well as a possible change in allocation policy to smaller, more nimble managers.

ADVANTAGES AND DISADVANTAGES OF A LARGE ASSET BASE

Advantages of a large asset base include more resources for research, increased ability to attract and retain investment talent, increased efficiency in brokerage, better access to companies, and greater bargaining power with broker/dealers.

However, challenges remain as to how to find alpha and identify the next generation of stars, which is a vital concern due to the fact that larger hedge funds also have significant disadvantages. Liquidity costs, for example, are significant, and smaller funds are able to put all of their money into their best ideas. Getting in and out of trades can be more difficult for the larger funds, especially with respect to their reduced ability to short. To compensate, suboptimal investment tactics may have to be adopted. Slippage also may occur with large orders.

Also worth noting are the psychological fears and career risks that can emerge as funds grow. Managers may test their limits by continuing to take in new money and increase their level of risk in an effort to boost returns. However, this may lead to growing concern over reputational risk, including possible dismissal or bankruptcy if the fund suffers. Organizational diseconomies are also evident. Managing money is different from managing people and managing a business, and the quality of personnel is difficult to maintain as fund size grows.

METHODOLOGY

Our study reviewed verifiable, "clean" data from 268 hedge funds in six strategies, each of which had monthly returns and assets under management continuously available for the time period of January 1995 through December 2002. Realizing that many past hedge fund studies traditionally have been incomplete, inaccurate, and prone to suffer from a number of biases, the research team focused on a small-sample size with the characteristics of a stratified sample from within the hedge fund universe. The sample included both funds that stopped reporting and funds that started operation during the same period, which ranged from January 1995 to December 2001.

With the goal of determining whether smaller funds outperformed larger funds, we measured three size-mimicking portfolios of equally weighted, monthly returns. We classified funds based on assets under management into three buckets, small (less than or equal to $50 million), medium ($50 million to $150 million), or large (more than $150 million).

Because assets under management are usually updated at year-end, the study measured performance beginning in January and then repeated the measurement each January thereafter for the duration of the study. Managers who entered the database during the year were allocated to one of three portfolios based on initial assets under management, and the portfolio was rebalanced accordingly. "Dead" funds remained in the portfolio until the month of their last reporting, at which time the portfolio was rebalanced to account for their exit.

DATA ANALYSIS

Table 5.1 provides the results that emerged when the sample of funds was allocated to three portfolios by size and results.

The evidence is clear. Size *does* impact performance. The emerging pattern, as shown in Table 5.1 and Figure 5.2, clearly supports the premise that smaller funds outperform larger funds. Thus our conclusion that size erodes returns.

However, the study also showed that midsize funds performed the worst, which suggests the concept of "midlife crisis" for hedge fund managers. Although smaller funds tend to outsource certain functions to presumably leading service providers and larger, institutionalized firms have top-tier processes, midsize firms tend to be in limbo in terms of the opportunities and processes required to attain optimum performance. (See Table 5.2.)

TABLE 5.1 Impact of Size on Performance

	Mean	(t stat)	St. Dev.	Skewness	Kurtosis	Jarque-Beta	# of Funds
Long/Short Equity							
Small	2.27	(6.73)	3.08	0.48	0.45	3.98	
Medium	1.19	(3.67)	2.97	0.48	3.80	53.90	
Large	1.39	(3.71)	3.44	−0.18	2.45	21.54	
All	1.77	(5.48)	2.97	0.38	0.99	5.48	60
Market Neutral							
Small	1.10	(10.02)	1.01	0.20	0.57	1.69	
Medium	0.65	(4.25)	1.40	−0.26	0.29	1.28	
Large	0.42	(2.55)	1.51	−1.03	4.41	83.26	
All	0.91	(9.36)	0.89	−0.12	0.11	0.25	54
Global Macro							
Small	1.16	(4.39)	2.43	0.12	−0.10	0.25	
Medium	1.00	(3.92)	2.33	0.41	0.46	3.07	
Large	1.98	(4.26)	4.27	0.09	0.51	1.03	
All	1.23	(4.83)	2.34	0.31	0.01	1.37	51
Convertible Arbitrage							
Small	1.61	(10.27	1.44	0.93	5.13	104.29	
Medium	1.04	(10.44)	0.91	−1.23	3.25	58.58	
Large	1.06	(9.99)	0.97	−1.95	6.88	219.26	
All	1.39	(11.51)	1.10	−0.39	3.33	40.88	30
Fixed Income							
Small	0.89	(9.64)	0.84	−1.30	4.43	92.43	
Medium	0.52	(4.04)	1.19	−1.58	4.39	102.35	
Large	0.92	(5.32)	1.59	1.04	7.93	235.55	
All	0.79	(8.28)	0.88	−2.06	8.02	284.87	44
Distressed							
Small	1.16	(6.25)	1.70	−1.10	6.64	171.57	
Medium	1.04	(6.12)	1.56	−0.18	2.95	31.02	
Large	0.73	(3.96)	1.69	−3.23	18.28	1315.55	
All	1.08	(6.64)	1.49	−1.76	8.27	282.94	29

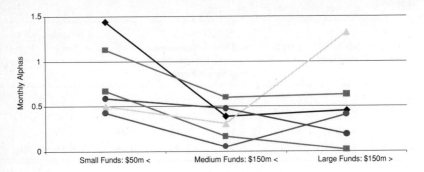

FIGURE 5.2   Size Erodes Performance.

Interesting to note is the fact that global macro managers proved to be the exception to the rule in this study as they were able to sustain performance regardless of size. These managers trade in different markets, maintain minimal infrastructure, and benefit from economies of scale.

Global macro has been in the spotlight recently as the changing pace of the global economies has led to traditional investors having a hard time coping with the correlation, or lack thereof, between the different markets across the world. In theory, global macro managers have the resources and skills to use sophisticated strategies to encompass all and profit from global trends, while traditional managers have limits on the style and scope of their investments.

We also evaluated results on a risk-adjusted basis and found that Sharpe ratios remained the same, as shown in Table 5.3.

TABLE 5.2   Medium Funds Suffer a Midlife Crisis

Mortality Rate	Small	Medium	Large
1 Year	3.48%	3.79%	2.03%
2 Years	8.45%	10.19%	2.78%
3 Years	11.81%	20.38%	2.86%
4 Years	18.93%	34.47%	3.57%
5 Years	23.69%	38.65%	3.57%
6 Years	27.22%	53.00%	3.57%
7 Years	32.00%	66.00%	3.57%

TABLE 5.3 Sharpe Ratio Data

	Unhedge Avg. SR	Beta Hedged	Hedged Beta/Sum	3 Factor	3 Factor/Sum Beta
Long/Short Equity					
Small	0.60	0.60	0.53	0.77	0.66
Medium	0.26	0.17	0.07	0.21	0.06
Large	0.28	0.19	0.11	0.30	0.20
All	0.46	0.43	0.31	0.62	0.42
Market Neutral					
Small	0.68	0.68	0.61	0.64	0.56
Medium	0.17	0.13	0.16	0.04	0.06
Large	0.01	0.02	0.05	0.00	0.03
All	0.56	0.55	0.53	0.48	0.46
Global Macro					
Small	0.31	0.24	0.18	0.30	0.23
Medium	0.25	0.16	0.12	0.16	0.11
Large	0.37	0.32	0.27	0.35	0.28
All	0.35	0.29	0.23	0.34	0.26
Convertible Arbitrage					
Small	0.83	0.81	0.52	0.87	0.55
Medium	0.69	0.67	0.43	0.67	0.42
Large	0.67	0.66	0.42	0.62	0.37
All	0.88	0.87	0.54	0.89	0.54
Fixed Income					
Small	0.56	0.53	0.47	0.52	0.45
Medium	0.09	0.04	−0.03	0.00	−0.08
Large	0.32	0.27	0.15	0.24	0.12
All	0.44	0.39	0.25	0.36	0.21
Distressed					
Small	0.44	0.38	0.27	0.37	0.27
Medium	0.40	0.34	0.22	0.41	0.28
Large	0.19	0.12	0.04	0.06	−0.02
All	0.45	0.39	0.25	0.42	0.26

Convertible arbitrage, an often-used hedge fund strategy that utilizes convertible securities as part of a diversified alternative investment portfolio, proved to be an exception to these findings, as smaller funds continued to show the same relative level of volatility as larger funds.

As background, consider that in its most basic form, arbitrage entails purchasing a convertible security and selling short the underlying stock to create a market-neutral position. Returns can be broken down into static return and dynamic return. Static return is generated by the receipt of a coupon or dividend in addition to the rebate on the short selling of the underlying stock, less any financing costs. The dynamic portion of the return is achieved when the arbitrageur dynamically hedges the position by buying or selling more or less of the underlying stock. Dynamic returns have comprised the largest portion of a convertible arbitrageur's performance in the last several years. This has certainly been the case more recently, in light of the high number of low-coupon-paying convertibles coming to market. However, the level of market volatility has been high, allowing arbitrageurs the opportunity to capture additional returns by altering the position's hedge ratio.

Estimates of volatility can be afflicted by the problem of "stale prices" that can be more severe with smaller funds than with larger ones.

With a fixed number of managers in place, putting a few more billion dollars to work might interfere with internal allocation infrastructure. This in turn can lead to creation of a special fund that specializes in emerging managers and may require a more in-depth, analytical due diligence process guided by a senior analyst and risk officer capable of making a judgment call. Ongoing due diligence is critical for a portfolio of smaller, emerging hedge funds, however, and the implications for portfolio construction are obvious.

Results of LJH's size versus performance study support the need to evaluate funds of all sizes when making hedge fund allocations.

TIPS

The tendency is often to invest using a "bigger is better" allocation strategy, yet the findings of a recent LJH study show that investors need to evaluate funds of all sizes when making hedge fund allocations. Small funds often tend to outperform as a result of their ability to put all of their money into their best ideas and because they have fewer constraints related to internal asset allocation guidelines. Before making a final decision on a hedge fund manager, we advise investors to consider the link between portfolio size and diminishing returns.

- Model an investment portfolio to insure proper diversification among strategies, but also pay heed to the fund's size.
- Bigger is not always better and investing with the large, high-profile funds may not always be the right move.
- Bias manager selection toward hedge funds that are nimble and responsive, and that generate alpha.
- Never forget the importance of relying on rigorous due diligence when selecting the best-performing managers, whether small, medium, or large.
- Consider the experiences of successful hedge fund managers who began with large funds, such as Tiger and Soros, but who subsequently left to start their own hedge funds, which closed to new investment at a smaller level.
- Investors in larger funds should watch the fund's ability to get in and out of trades and their possible reduced ability to short. This may lead to the adoption of suboptimal investment tactics and/or possible slippage with large orders.
- Monitor the activities of the hedge fund manager as fund size increases; some may take in new money and increase their level of risk in an effort to boost returns.
- Know the people at the fund since quality of personnel may be difficult to maintain as fund size grows.

- Midsize funds, which appear to often be in limbo, performed the worst in this study, which suggests the concept of midlife crisis for hedge fund managers.
- Global macro managers are the exception to the rule in this study; they proved their ability to sustain performance regardless of size, probably due to the markets in which they trade and economies of scale.

Directional Investing through Global Macros and Managed Futures

Global macro and managed futures investing are two forms of directional or opportunistic investing strategies that investors should consider when determining which strategies to include in their hedge fund portfolio. Each represents a unique opportunity to profit from global economic markets and trading in commodities with strong upside value.

Because of the instruments in which they most commonly trade, these two strategies have an organizational structure that is distinct from the conventional hedge fund limited partnership or limited liability corporation. Both strategies trade in commodities or commodities-related derivatives through what is known as a commodity trading advisor (CTA).

INSIDE THE GLOBAL MACRO STRATEGY

Traditional investment strategies, whether they are geographically limited or stylistically limited, have produced outstanding results some of the time but may fall short in terms of long-run consistency. To make up for the lack of diversity, global macro funds have positioned themselves so they have the ability to help their investors to capitalize on opportunities in any environment.

Global macro managers who run large, highly diversified portfolios that are designed to profit from major shifts in global capital flows, interest rates, and currencies are worthy of investors' consideration. These funds represent the purest form of a top-down approach to absolute return investing and pursue an opportunistic top-down approach based on shifts in global economies.

Finding a global macro hedge fund manager with the capacity to take in new investment may present a challenge. Compared to other strategies, global macro funds make up a small fraction of the hedge fund world. It is interesting to note, however, that although global macro hedge funds are still small in terms of the number of funds, the strategy tends to include the largest funds in terms of assets under management. Several of the best-known hedge fund managers, such as George Soros and Julian Robertson, are identified with this strategy. The strategy continues to grow despite the fact that historically it has been viewed by some investors as less favorable than those whose investment range is limited to seemingly stable economies, such as those of the United States and western Europe. Investors will continue to hear more about the global macro strategy in the months and years ahead. (See Table 6.1.)

TABLE 6.1   Global Macro Strategy Overview

- Managers have the broadest investment mandate of any of the hedge fund strategies.
- Their approach is general rather than specific.
- Managers use top-down, macroeconomic analysis to invest on a leveraged basis across multiple sectors, markets, instruments, and trading styles.
- Timing is everything.
- Managers have flexibility and objectivity to move from opportunity to opportunity and trend to trend.
- Asset size per fund is the largest in the hedge fund industry.
- Managers earn returns by identifying where in the economy the risk premium has swung farthest from equilibrium, investing in that situation, and recognizing when the extraordinary conditions that made that particular approach so profitable have deteriorated or been counteracted by a new trend in the opposite direction.
- The art of macro investing lies in determining when a process has been stretched to its inflection point[a] and when to become involved in its trend back to equilibrium.

[a]Inflection point: Point at which an extreme valuation reverses itself, usually marked or signaled by a major policy move.

To understand the interworkings of the global macro strategy, investors should know that managers speculate on changes in countries' economic policies and shifts in currency and interest rates via derivatives and the use of leverage. Portfolios tend to be highly concentrated in a small number of investment themes, which typically involve large bets on the relative valuations of two asset categories. Global macro managers structure complex combinations of investments to benefit from the narrowing or widening of the valuation spreads between these assets in such a way as to maximize the potential return and minimize potential losses. In some instances, the investments are designed specifically to take advantage of artificial imbalances in the marketplace brought on by central bank activities.

As the changing pace of the global economies continues to occupy the spotlight, investors are having a hard time coping with the correlation, or lack thereof, between the different markets of the world. In theory, global macro managers have the resources and skills to use sophisticated strategies to profit from global trends. They are able to take advantage of more opportunities than traditional asset managers who have limits on the style and scope of their investments.

To profit from the impact of market moves, global macro hedge funds often use leverage and derivatives, strategies used by less than 5 percent of hedge funds. The primary focus of most hedge funds is to produce consistent returns and then focus on the magnitude of those returns; the emphasis is on quality, not quantity. Most use derivatives only for hedging or not at all, and do not use leverage. Some hedge fund strategies, such as those used by funds investing in special situations, arbitrage, or distressed securities, are not correlated to equity markets and are thus able to deliver consistent returns with a low risk of capital loss. Past results indicate that a diversified portfolio of hedge funds delivers more consistent returns than pure equity or bond investments. Investors who might otherwise benefit from hedge funds end up making investments that are more volatile, less conservative, and riskier than many hedge funds—through a lack of knowledge and experience on their own part or on the part of their financial advisors.

This vast availability of investment vehicles creates unique challenges and presents several key questions. To simplify the myriad of possible questions, consider whether it is possible for a global macro manager to trade effectively with all aspects of global markets in mind. The traditional investor thought superior profits could be made by utilizing specific strategies or locations. This was true in the past due to the high correlation of many of the world's markets. When markets show low correlation, trends will have to be exploited in their initial environment rather than waiting for the swell to reach secondary markets; this trend is a temporary state that should balance out over time and eventually lead to a rise in market correlations.

To understand the desirability of the global macro fund, investors must understand the different geographical and political segments and the art of combining them. Once these trends or opportunities are recognized, it becomes evident that the global macro strategy is the only one that has the ability to encompass all individual opportunities, without limitation, to produce noncorrelated consistent results.

History has been a continuation of world conflicts that have shaped and molded the economic landscape both on a short-term cyclical basis as well as a longer-term secular outlook. Over the 60-plus years since 1941, the world landscape has been a continuation of wars: World War II, the Korean War, the Vietnam War, the Cold War, the Persian Gulf War, and most recently, the Iraq War. With the rise of Asia, the European Economic Community (EEC), and the freeing of former communist economies has come an economic war for capital and resources. Throughout each of these conflicts, investment volatility and opportunities have existed across markets and assets. Those who are well positioned to benefit are typically flexible and opportunistic, taking advantage of opportunities wherever they presented themselves.

The unprecedented rise in equity markets during the last few years has provided such an opportunity. Investors have reaped the benefits of these rampant global markets, which have coincided with falling interest rates and strong growth. This enormous bull market has created an environment of lofty equity market expectations. Going forward, nonequity assets will be the generator, as we see a drop in the demand for goods and an increase in demand for nonproductive capital. In this environment, bonds, currencies, and commodities will outperform equities.

The International Monetary Fund and the world community will continue to be called on to contribute nonproductive capital to ensure the viability of Far Eastern countries, draining liquidity and credit from the system. This strain on the system, coupled with the slow process of Europe to fundamentally change its system to address high unemployment and slow growth, creates a negative wave that even the relatively strong U.S. economy cannot truly avoid in its truly global financial system. This ripple effect has appeared in recent U.S. corporate earnings reports, as foreign demand drops and the ability to raise prices diminishes, putting a squeeze on profits and pressure on the equity markets.

Slow growth, low inflation, and a potential deflationary environment create an economic backdrop in which a shift in the allocation of capital can be seen to nonequity asset classes, such as bonds, currencies, and commodities. Investment opportunities and volatility have always existed and are likely to persist, providing investors who have a macro view with the ability to thrive. The current environment is a very positive one for those who can move from market to market and asset to asset, as the most attractive opportunities shift in these global capital markets.

MANAGED FUTURES

Managed futures (see Table 6.2) investing involves trading in futures contracts on a wide range of commodities and financial derivatives, and essentially represents an efficient means of introducing commodities-related investing into an investment portfolio. Approximately $86.5 billion is invested in managed futures today, a number that has expanded tremendously over the last 20 years and that represents a 70 percent gain to date, according to a recent study by the Barclay Trading Group. As is the case with hedge funds overall, this growth is largely attributable to institutional investors such as pensions, endowments, and banks, but lower minimum investment levels are also attracting more high-net-worth investors than ever.

For investors to fully understand how to benefit from the managed futures strategy, they must understand the difference between hedgers and speculators, the two distinct categories of individuals who transact in futures markets. Hedgers are those who use futures contracts to protect against price movements in an underlying asset that they either buy or sell in the ordinary course of business. For example, farmers who rely

TABLE 6.2 Managed Futures Defined

Characteristics of Managed Futures Funds

- Dynamic enough to participate directly in many sectors of the world economy
  - ☐ Currencies and indices (stocks and others)
  - ☐ Credit instruments and petroleum products
  - ☐ Grains and seeds, livestock and meats
  - ☐ Food, fiber, metals
- Noncorrelation to broader markets and trends, in both up and down market cycle
- Outlook is strong, given the trend toward globalization of world economies

Potential Benefits of Managed Futures

- Positive returns not directly tied to stock or bond markets
- Ability to profit in any economic environment
- Portfolio diversification
- Monthly liquidity

on one crop for all of their revenue cannot afford a sharp decline in the price of the crop before it is sold. Therefore, the farmers would sell a futures contract that specifies the amount, grade, price, and date of delivery of the crop, effectively reducing the risk that the crop price will decline before it is harvested and sold. Speculators have no intention of physical settlement of the underlying asset; rather, they simply are seeking short-term gains from the expected fluctuation in futures prices. Most futures trading activity is, in fact, conducted by speculators, who use futures markets (as opposed to transacting directly in the commodity) because it allows them to take a significant position with reasonably low transaction costs and a high amount of leverage. (See Table 6.3.)

TABLE 6.3 Managed Futures Profit in Both Up and Down Markets

Managed futures have the potential to be profitable in any type of economic climate because the trading advisors have the flexibility to go long (buy in anticipation of rising prices) or short (sell in anticipation of declining prices).

This ability to go long or short gives managed funds the potential to profit (or lose) in times of:

- Energy abundance or crisis
- Economic strength or weakness
- Political stability or upheaval
- Inflationary or deflationary times

Managed futures investors participate in this speculative trading by investing with a CTA. Although hedge funds that engage in futures trading are considered to be managed futures investors, they differ from private pools and public funds in that futures are not the core of their strategy, rather are a single component of a synthesis of instruments. Managed futures portfolios can be structured for a single investor or for a group of investors. Portfolios that cater to a single investor are known as individually managed accounts. Typically these accounts are structured for institutions and high-net-worth individuals. As mentioned, managed futures portfolios that are structured for a group of investors are referred to as either private commodity pools or public commodity funds. Public funds, often run by leading brokerage firms, are offered to retail clients and often carry lower investment minimums combined with higher fees. Private pools are the more popular structure for group investors. Like individually managed accounts, they attract institutional and high-net-worth capital. Private pools in the United States tend to be structured as limited partnerships where the general partner is a commodity pool operator (CPO) and serves as the sponsor/salesperson for the fund. In addition to selecting the CTA(s) to actively manage the portfolio, the CPO is responsible for monitoring their performance and determining compliance with the pool's policy statement.

The evidence supporting managed futures and other alternative investment strategies should not be surprising. Advantages of managed futures investing include:

- Low to negative correlation to equities and other hedge funds
- Negative correlation to equities and hedge funds during periods of poor performance
- Diversified opportunities, in both markets and manager styles
- Substantial market liquidity
- Transparency of positions and profits/losses
- Multilayer level of regulatory oversight

Investors who have historically been long only in equity and fixed-income markets have experienced periods of positive performance and periods of negative performance. The ability to take long or short positions in futures markets creates the potential to profit whether markets are rising or falling. Due to the wide array of noncorrelated markets available for futures investing, there can be a bull market in one area and a bear market in another. For example, U.S. soybean prices may be rising while the Japanese yen is falling. Both of these occurrences offer the potential to gain. However, it is important to realize that as a speculative investment strategy, managed futures investing is best pursued as a long-term strategy. Because of the strategy's cyclical nature, it should not be relied on as a short-term investment strategy. Indeed, most experts recommend a minimum three-year investment.

According to CTAs who use global futures and options markets as an investment medium, managed futures investing differs from hedge fund and mutual fund investing in a number of fundamental ways, including transparency, liquidity, regulatory oversight, and the use of exchanges. These underlying distinctions provide support for adding managed futures investments to a portfolio that includes both traditional and alternative investments.

Because futures contracts are by definition traded on organized exchanges across the globe, the bid and offer prices on specific contracts are publicly quoted. Consequently, investors can ascertain the current value and calculate the gain or loss on outstanding positions with relative ease. Additionally, open interest—the number of contracts currently outstanding on a particular asset—are quoted as well. In contrast, hedge funds often engage in transactions involving esoteric over-the-counter (OTC) derivatives, whose market values may not be readily available. This fact potentially can inhibit the manager's ability to effectively monitor positions.

Again, the exchange-based nature of futures contracts plays a significant role in how the strategy functions. Positions can be entered into and exited continuously, regardless of size. When a CTA believes that a large position needs to be liquidated to avoid huge losses, timing is critical. Sometimes a hedge fund may have significant positions in a particular type of instrument that it wishes to unload due to adverse market conditions, but the illiquidity of that particular market may inhibit it from doing so. The point is that liquidity allows CTAs to reduce and/or eliminate significant positions during periods of sharp declines.

Like any investment strategy, managed futures have some short-comings. The strategy's disadvantages may include:

- A high degree of volatility
- High fees
- A low level of advisor attention

As a stand-alone investment, managed futures tend to be highly volatile, producing uneven cash flows to the investor because annual returns are heavily generated by sharp, sudden movements in futures prices. Because the nature of this strategy is based primarily on such movements, returns undoubtedly will continue to be volatile. However, managed futures are not typically chosen as a stand-alone investment. Rather, they are selected as a single component of a diversified portfolio. Due to their historically low correlation with other alternative investments, their volatility actually can reduce the overall risk of the portfolio. Investors also have complained about the lack of advisor attention to the customized fit of managed futures into their portfolio. Due to the many different styles and markets of managed futures investing, investors certainly can benefit from specialized attention. In this light, consulting services can be truly beneficial to portfolio. Not only can a consultant offer clients a careful understanding of their investment objectives, but he or she also provides clients with comfort in the fact that careful due diligence of CTAs has been performed. Due to the wide dispersion of CTA performance, this factor can be of paramount importance.

The basis for the managed futures strategy—as well as the strategy for traditional securities—is that CTAs typically rely on either technical or fundamental analysis, or a combination of both, for their trading decisions. Technical analysis is derived from the theory that a study of the markets themselves can reveal valuable information that can be used to predict future commodity prices. Such information includes actual daily, weekly, and monthly price fluctuations, volume variations, and changes in open interest. Technical traders often utilize charts and sophisticated computer models to analyze these items.

In contrast, to predict future prices, fundamental analysis relies on the study of external factors that affect the supply and demand of a particular commodity. Such factors include the nature of the economy, governmental policies, domestic and foreign political events, and the weather. Fundamental analysis is predicated on the notion that, over time, the price (actual value) of a futures contract must reflect the value of the underlying commodity (perceived value) and, further, that the value of the underlying commodity is based on these external variables. The fundamental trader profits from the convergence of perceived value and actual value.

Within the specific realm of managed futures investing, CTAs employ three general classifications of methodologies: (1) discretionary, (2) systematic trends, and (3) followers. However, in practice these categories tend to overlap.

Discretionary advisors, in their purest form, rely on fundamental research and analytics to determine trade executions. For example, a fundamental advisor may come to understand that severe weather conditions have reduced the estimate for the supply of wheat this season. Basic rules of supply and demand dictate that the price of wheat (and, hence, wheat futures) should rise in this circumstance. Whereas the systematic trader would wait until these fundamental data are reflected in the futures price before trading, the pure discretionary advisor immediately trades on this information. Few advisors are purely discretionary; rather, almost all of them rely on systems to some extent because there simply is too much information for diversified advisors to digest to make sound trading decisions. For example, discretionary advisors may use automated information to spot trends and judgment to determine position size. Another possibility is that after deciding to make a trade based on fundamental research, discretionary advisors may analyze technical data to confirm their opinions and determine entry and exit points. The main distinction between discretionary and systematic advisors is that discretionary advisors do not rely primarily on a computerized model to execute trades.

The main argument against discretionary advisors is that they incorporate emotion into their trades. Like other investment strategies, managed futures investing is only as successful as the discipline of the manager to adhere to its requirements in the face of market adversity. Given the nature of extreme volatility often found in managed futures trading, discretionary traders may subject their decisions to behavioral biases. Another argument is that the heavy reliance on individual knowledge and focus creates a serious investment risk. The ability of the advisor to avoid ancillary distractions becomes paramount when the CTA uses discretionary tactics.

Systematic advisors lie at the opposite extreme. These advisors use sophisticated computerized models, often referred to as a black box, that typically include neural nets or complex algorithms to dictate trading activity. Advisors differ in what factors they use as inputs into their models and how their models interpret given factors. Some systematic advisors design systems that analyze historical price relationships, probability measures, or statistical data to identify trading opportunities; however, the majority rely to some extent on trend following.

For a trade entry signal, systematic advisors rely on technical data, such as price patterns, current price relative to historical price, price volatility, volume, and open interest. Profitable positions may be closed out based on one of these signals, if a trend reversal is identified, or if the end of a trend is signaled based on an overbought/oversold situation. Some systematic advisors use a single-system approach. However, others employ multiple systems that can operate either in tandem or in mutual exclusivity. An example of a multisystem approach operating in tandem is when one system generates a buy signal and the other system indicates a flat or sell signal. The result will be no trade because both systems are not in agreement. Systems that operate independently would each execute a trade based on the respective signal. The main advantage of a multisystem approach is diversification of signals.

Although systematic trading effectively removes the emotional element from trade execution, the use of a systematic methodology does not imply that there is a human disconnect. On the contrary, the systems typically are developed and monitored by humans with extensive trading experience. In addition, although specific market entry and exit points usually are determined by the system, human discretion often is included in decisions such as portfolio weightings, position size, entry into new markets, stop losses, margin/equity ratios, and selection of contract months.

The final classification of methodologies is trend following, which is a method of trading that seeks to establish and maintain market positions based on the emergence of major price trends through an analysis of market price movement and other statistical analyses. This technique is consistent with the underlying concept of managed futures investing, which is that prices move from equilibrium to a transitory stage and back to equilibrium. Trend followers attempt to capture this divergence of prices through the detection of various signals. Although trend followers may employ computerized systems or rely on human judgment to identify trends, they typically choose the former. As a result, trend followers often are classified in the general category of systematic advisors.

A common misconception about trend followers is that they attempt to time the market perfectly—that is, entering and exiting markets at the most favorable prices. On the contrary, trend followers are reactionary—they do not attempt to predict a trend; rather, they respond to an existing trend. Generally, they seek to close out losing positions quickly and hold profitable positions as long as the market trend is perceived to exist. Consequently, the number of losing contracts may vastly exceed the number of profitable contracts; however, the gains on the favorable positions are expected to more than offset the losses on losing contracts.

Because of the breadth of markets and instruments that any given managed futures fund might be involved in, it is not possible to identify common risk factors to be ascribed to the whole sector. However, there are common approaches to risk management that obtain at a general level to all CTAs.

Commodity trading advisors can diversify in a number of ways, such as trading different markets or employing different strategies or systems. Trading programs often employ risk management systems, which serve to determine and limit the equity committed to each trade, each market, and each account. For example, the risk management system of one CTA attempts to limit risk exposure to any one commodity to 1 percent of the total portfolio and to any one commodity group to 3 percent of the total portfolio.

Unprofitable positions often are closed out through the use of stop losses, where every position in a program has a price associated with it that, if hit, will result in executing orders to close out the positions. Stop losses are designed to limit the downside risk on any given position. They can be based on price stops, time stops, volatility stops, and the like.

The easiest way to think of leverage is as the ratio of face market value of all the investments in the portfolio to the equity in the account. A common misconception is that leverage is bad; an example of a good use of leverage is to lever markets with less movement to match volatilities across a portfolio. In other words, the manager is equalizing risk across the opportunities within that portfolio. The amount of leverage will then change over time based on ongoing research, program volatility, current market volatility, risk exposure, or manager discretion. For example, during periods of high volatility, a manager often reduces the amount of leverage because the total number of contracts needed to satisfy the position has been reduced. Also, managers often decrease leverage during periods of declining profit to preserve capital and limit losses. There is no standard of leverage; however, in general, CTAs use leverage as a multiple of between three to six times capital.

Regardless of the chosen methodology, managed futures investments can be short, medium, or long term. Short-term trades typically last between 3 to 5 days, but can be as short as intraday or as long as 1 month. Intermediate trades, on average, last 12 weeks; long-term trades typically exceed 9 months.

Managers focusing on short-term trades try to capture rapid moves and are out of the market more than their intermediate- and long-term counterparts. Because these managers base their activity on swift fluctuation in prices, their returns tend to be noncorrelated to those of long-term or general advisors as well as to each other. In addition, they are more sensitive to transaction costs and rely heavily on liquidity and high volatility for returns. Strong trending periods, which often exceed the short-term time frame, tend to hamper the returns of these advisors and favor those with a longer time horizon.

The fact that managed futures investments are low to negatively correlated with fixed-income and equity asset classes, as well as other hedge fund strategies provides support for managed futures as a diversification vehicle.

Like a portfolio of equities, multimanaged CTA portfolios benefit from increased diversification. Investors seeking to gain from the benefits of managed futures can lower their risk by investing in a diversified portfolio of managed futures advisors. Of course, the number of managers to include in a particular portfolio depends on the current diversification of that portfolio—for example, its current allocation to stocks and bonds. It also depends on the percentage of capital that the investor is willing to commit to managed futures. An investor seeking to commit 30 percent of a diversified portfolio to managed futures would want to employ more managers than an investor only looking for 5 percent exposure. These same investors then would want to analyze their current portfolio weightings of traditional and alternative investments before determining how many managers to whom they will allocate capital. Given that there are different styles (i.e., discretionary and systematic) as well as diversified futures markets (i.e., commodities, financials, and currencies), diversification can be accomplished with relative ease. It is worth noting, however, that there tends to be a high degree of correlation between trend-following managers. Although these managers may be utilizing completely different techniques to make trading decisions, essentially they are still relying on a common source of value to make profits.

As more sophisticated investors become aware of the noncorrelated nature of managed futures to hedge funds and equities, asset growth into this category is expected to continue to increase. Institutional participation will continue to grow as a result of the increased use of insurance products and investable hedge fund indices. Increased use of equity trading may become prevalent, as the performance of managed futures still lags the S&P. Overall, increased globalization should result in more opportunities for managed futures investors.

To fully appreciate the distinction between CTAs and hedge funds, it is helpful to examine the Commodity Futures Trading Commission (CFTC), created by Congress in 1974 as an independent agency with the mandate to regulate commodity futures and option markets in the United States. The agency protects market participants against manipulation, abusive trade practices, and fraud. Essentially, the CFTC is to the world of commodities and futures trading what the SEC is to the traditional securities markets. The commission performs three primary functions: (1) contract review, (2) market surveillance, and (3) regulation of futures professionals.

All CTAs must be registered with the CFTC, file detailed disclosure documents, and be members of the National Futures Association (NFA), a self-regulatory organization approved by the commission. The CFTC also seeks to protect customers by requiring:

- Registrants to disclose market risks and past performance information to prospective customers
- That customer funds be kept in accounts separate from those maintained by the firm for its own use
- That customer accounts to be adjusted to reflect the current market value at the close of trading each day (marked to market)

In addition, the CFTC monitors registrant supervision systems, internal controls, and sales practice compliance programs. Last, all registrants are required to complete ethics training.

Additionally, the NFA serves to protect investors by maintaining the integrity of the marketplace. The association screens those who wish to conduct business with the investing public, develops a wide range of investor protection rules, and monitors all of its members for compliance. The NFA also provides investors with a fast, efficient method for settling disputes when they occur.

An additional layer of investor protection is provided by the exchanges on which CTAs trade, which have rules that cover trade clearance, trade orders and records, position and price limits, disciplinary actions, floor trading practices, and standards of business conduct. Although an exchange primarily operates autonomously, the CFTC must approve any rule additions or amendments. Exchanges also are regularly audited by the CFTC to verify that their compliance programs are operating effectively.

In 2002 Congress passed the Commodity Futures Modernization Act, which includes a hard look at derivatives clearing organizations, rules governing margins for security futures, and dual trading by floor brokers. In addition, the agency embarked on a massive review of energy trading in the wake of the Enron scandal. A comprehensive risk management assessment is also an agency focus. To further protect investors, the provisions of the USA Patriot Act now require certain registered CTAs to establish anti-money-laundering provisions.

TIPS

The potential to profit from global economic markets and trading in commodities with strong upside value makes a compelling case for an investment in the global macro and managed futures strategies. Both are directional or opportunistic strategies that are increasing in popularity because of their potential to provide long-term consistency and balance to a portfolio.

Global Macro

- Learn more about how global macro hedge fund managers speculate on various countries' dynamic economic policies and take advantage of global trends.
- Consider investing with a global macro manager who runs a diversified portfolio that is able to profit from major shifts in global capital flows, interest rates, and currencies.
- Monitor the global macro funds' use of leverage and derivatives to profit from the impact of market moves, which represent strategies used by less than 5 percent of hedge funds.
- Study how history has molded today's economic landscape, and how investment volatility and opportunities have existed across markets and assets.
- Learn how the current environment is positive for those who can move from market to market and asset to asset, as the most attractive opportunities shift in these global capital markets.

Managed Futures

- Include managed futures investing, which involves trading in futures contracts, as an efficient way to utilize commodity-related investing in an investment portfolio.
- Invest with a commodity trading advisor who can take a significant position with reasonably low transaction costs and a high amount of leverage

- Consider whether you need a managed futures portfolio that is an individually managed account structured for a single investor, or whether you should be part of a group of investors in a private commodity pool or public commodity fund, the latter of which is available from leading brokerage firms at lower minimum investment levels.
- Pursue managed futures investing as a long-term strategy, because of its cyclical nature.
- Understand that managed futures investing has different standards from other types of hedge fund investing with respect to transparency, liquidity, regulatory oversight, and exchange usage, and consider whether this strategy will work for you.
- Know the difference between black box systematic traders and discretionary traders.

CHAPTER 7

Profiting from the Corporate Life Cycle

This chapter will help investors understand the two most common event-driven hedge fund strategies, risk arbitrage, and distressed securities investing. The event-driven category is defined as strategies that seek to profit principally from the occurrence of some of the typical events that occur in a corporate life cycle, such as mergers, acquisitions, spin-offs, restructurings, and recapitalizations. (See Figure 7.1.)

In addition to risk arbitrage and distressed securities funds, the event-driven strategy includes funds that are best classified as focusing on special situations, although both risk arbitrageurs and distressed securities funds frequently get involved in activities that do not fall conveniently within the mainstream definition of either strategy.

BETTING ON A TAKEOVER THROUGH MERGER (RISK) ARBITRAGE

Investors in merger arbitrage, also called risk arbitrage, invest through hedge fund managers who take a long position in the target company of an announced takeover bid. In combination, where the consideration is the stock of the acquirer, the arbitrageur generally will sell that stock short. This strategy is analogous to the insurance business in that the arbitrageur is insuring existing shareholders against the risk of the deal not taking place. The spread between the market price and the offer

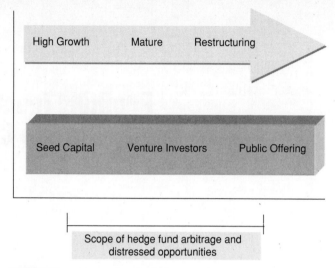

FIGURE 7.1   Corporate Life Cycle.

price is the equivalent of the insurance premium, which will be the return to the arbitrageur should the deal proceed to completion.

The risk arbitrage strategy should be considered as part of an overall allocation to alternative investments because it provides benefits such as low market correlation and a low standard deviation to an efficient, diversified portfolio. In addition, risk arbitrage funds have returned consistently strong profits to their investors for an extended period of time, independent of overall market conditions.

Successful managers are experts at analyzing deals and taking into account any possible regulatory obstacles and downside risks should the deal fail to materialize. The possibility that the deal might not proceed to completion is the key risk; and if managers have a strong view that a deal will not proceed to completion, they can short the stock of the target company, an act that is known as a Chinese. The potential reward in such cases is substantial, but constitutes only a small percentage of total positions entered.

Risk arbitrage fund managers focus on companies involved in mergers or acquisitions to take advantage of pricing inefficiencies in the shares of those companies. Fund managers can take long and short positions in both companies involved in a sale or merger to make profits. Typically, arbitrageurs are long the stock of the company being acquired and short the acquiring company.

A typical example of how risk arbitrage managers pursue returns follows. When a company announces its intent to acquire or merge with another company, typically there is a spread between the current market price of the shares and the price to be paid for the shares in the deal, because acquiring companies usually offer more than the current market price to encourage the deal. At the time of the announcement, the price of the target company rises to approach the offer price of the deal, yet it will stop short of the offer price to reflect the uncertainty that the deal will go through.

Risk arbitrage fund managers look to lock in this spread as a hedged profit by going long and short in the appropriate shares. When the deal is a trade of securities, the manager can lock in the spread by going long in the stock of the target company and selling short the stock of the acquiring company, which is done in case the purchaser's stock price falls. If the offer in the deal is a cash offer for stock, the manager simply goes long in the stock of the acquired company, without the need to short the acquiring company.

The greatest risk facing event-driven strategies is when the anticipated event driving an investment fails to materialize. In the case of risk arbitrage funds, this situation happens when an announced merger or acquisition fails to be completed. Should the deal not be completed, the stock price of the company being acquired will fall and significant losses could occur for the arbitrage fund. Regulatory considerations are one of the possible reasons for a deal to fall through. When two publicly traded companies have entered into a deal, there is always the possibility that antitrust regulators may disallow an acquisition after a review. One example is when the European Union (EU) rejected the proposed merger of General Electric and Honeywell in 2001. Merger arbitrageurs specialize in evaluating this risk to minimize the losses that can occur when deals are not completed. Risk arbitrage managers also create diversified portfolios of merger activity so as to reduce such specific event risk. (See Figure 7.2.)

M&A Activity: Company B (the buyer) annouces offer to acquire
Company T (the target) at a share price of $110

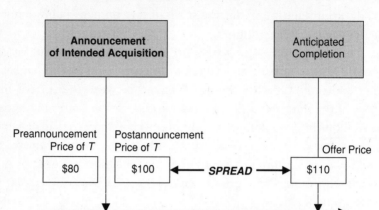

- Fund managers take a long position in the stock of a company being acquired in a merger, leveraged buyout, or takeover and a simultaneous short position in the stock of the acquiring company.

- If the takeover fails, this strategy may result in large losses; if it is successful, it can result in large gains.

- Often risk is reduced by avoiding hostile takeovers and by investing only in deals that are announced.

FIGURE 7.2   Merger Arbitrage Example.

The level of risk undertaken by each arbitrage fund manager varies. Some managers invest only in officially announced transactions, whereas others undertake a higher level of risk by investing in positions at an earlier stage, such as in rumored deals. Transactions undertaken at an earlier stage offer a wider spread and therefore greater returns to compensate for the increased risk. (See Figure 7.3.)

Most managers use a formal methodology in evaluating potential risk. Quality research by fund managers and their staffs is an integral part of the process and helps to reduce risk. A diversified portfolio containing a large share of the transaction universe also helps managers to reduce risk further. (See Figure 7.4.)

In recent years risk arbitrage funds have proven to be consistently strong performers, even during periods of volatile market swings.

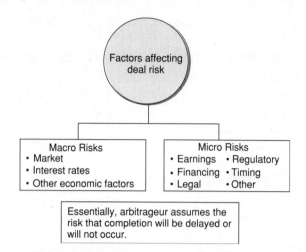

FIGURE 7.3   Potential Risks in Merger Arbitrage.

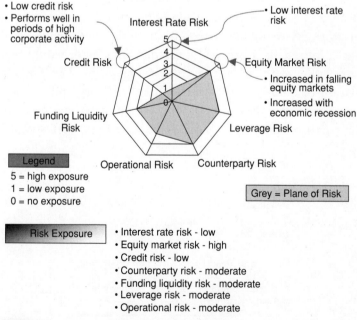

FIGURE 7.4   Merger (Risk) Arbitrage Risk Profile.

Although returns for merger arbitrage funds were outpaced by the Standard & Poor's (S&P) 500 during the broad market's bull run of the 1980s and 1990s, merger arbitrageurs still were successful in generating steady returns. One of the main attractions of this strategy is the supposed low correlation to the equity markets; stock-specific events are expected to be the main driver of performance, rather than directional movements in the equity markets.

INVESTING IN DISTRESSED SECURITIES

Until recently, investors have overlooked distressed securities, and the strategy is just now outgrowing its reputation as one of the most misunderstood segments of the hedge fund universe. One reason some investors have not appreciated the opportunities to profit from distressed securities investing is that investing in businesses experiencing financial distress does not have the appeal of other investment strategies. The results, however, more than make up for what it lacks in glamour and continue to lead more investors into this strategy.

Distressed securities funds regularly produce exceptional investment returns with relatively low volatility. In addition to being good risk-adjusted investments, distressed securities funds have exhibited a very low correlation to the performance of the broad market. The very low correlation of distressed securities with the equity and fixed-income markets can be explained by their transaction-based nature, which for the most part operates independently of the current status of the mar-

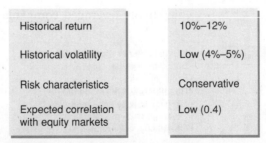

Historical return	10%–12%
Historical volatility	Low (4%–5%)
Risk characteristics	Conservative
Expected correlation with equity markets	Low (0.4)

FIGURE 7.5   Risk arbitrage at a glance.
Source: LJH Global Investments, LLC.

ket. Such low correlations make the distressed securities strategy an excellent fit as part of a well-diversified portfolio. (See Figure 7.5.)

Distressed securities had an exceptional run in 2003 with the HFRI Distressed Securities Index posting returns of 20.9 percent for the year. The large postrecession supply of distressed companies followed by low interest rates, favorable tax law changes, fiscal stimulus, and positive gross domestic product growth provided the most favorable conditions for the strategy since 1996. Even as interest rates increased midyear 2003, investors searching for yield continued to provide the driver for many distressed securities managers to continue to generate returns until year-end.

The bear market years of 2000 to 2002 only accelerated this process. The bursting of the stock market bubble, the recession, widespread corporate fraud, restatements of performance, and the impact of terrorism on the travel industries resulted in motivated selling by institutions managing credit exposure and losses and created significant market dislocations and attractive pricing. Record levels of bankruptcy filings, debt restructurings, and junk bond issuance in the United States in recent years are a primary cause of today's active secondary market in distressed securities. All in all, the increase in overall supply and diversity of distressed corporate and small balance loan situations is higher than investors have ever witnessed.

Overall, we believe that the distressed sectors will perform well in the next few years as inflationary pressures push interest rates higher. Performance for the strategy is not expected to repeat the high levels of 2003, but should still be respectable. We think investors should focus on experienced managers who have been active in this strategy over the past several years with a proven ability to maneuver through a less favorable capital market environment. Highly leveraged companies that are not successful at fixing their operational problems could very well experience cash flow problems and may be unable to deleverage if access to the capital markets diminishes. Additionally, manufacturing companies hurt by import substitutions or increased energy costs could be excluded from the economic recovery. Distressed securities managers will need to be cognizant of the potential for a wide variety of colliding trends—rising interest rates, falling currency costs, and rising energy costs—that may impact the capital markets going forward, making investment opportunities less plentiful and more difficult to identify. This fact again points to the need for investors to exercise expert due diligence and insist on intelligent transparency.

Today's market is unique in both size and scope, including a broad spectrum of distressed claims such as bank loans, debentures, trade payables, private placements, real estate mortgages, legal damage claims, and rejected lease contracts.

Distressed securities hedge funds invest specifically in the securities of companies that are experiencing financial or operational difficulties. The term "distressed securities" refers to a wide range of financial claims on firms that either have filed for bankruptcy protection or are trying to avoid bankruptcy by negotiating an out-of-court restructuring with their creditors.

The recovery process of distressed companies generally involves several major steps, and distressed securities managers may focus on specific areas in this process by extracting value when a catalyst or an event that changes the price of the securities of the distressed companies occurs. Hedge fund managers who specialize in distressed securities blend a specialized knowledge of the bankruptcy process with fundamental analysis of distressed companies and the intrinsic value of their debt securities and equities that allows them to predict, and when necessary take actions to influence, the outcome of the bankruptcies and reorganizations.

Distressed securities managers typically invest long and short in the securities of companies undergoing bankruptcy or reorganization. They tend to focus on companies that are undergoing financial rather than operational distress—in other words, good companies with bad balance sheets. Overleveraged companies that cannot cover their debt burden become oversold when institutional bondholders liquidate their holdings; as a result, as the companies enter bankruptcy, distressed securities managers buy the positions at pennies on the dollar. Often the securities of these companies trade below their inherent value because of the uncertainty of the companies' future. Furthermore, traditional investors often are restricted from owning the securities of companies with very low credit ratings. As a result, hedge fund managers often can buy securities of sound companies with real assets that have not, for a variety of technical reasons, been able to access the capital markets and deleverage their balance sheets. Managers then look for the instruments to appreciate or be exchanged for higher-valued securities at various points as the company works its way through the restructuring process. Some fund managers also hedge their portfolio by selling short the securities of companies they believe will not restructure successfully and head toward bankruptcy, as well as those that will not emerge from bankruptcy.

Distressed managers usually concentrate on certain sectors and investing styles that fit their own expertise. Aspects that differentiate distressed investing styles include the type of claim instrument invested in (i.e., bank debt, corporate debt, trade claims, and equities), the phase of the bankruptcy process, and the exit strategy used. Although the specific approaches are as diverse as the instruments and companies in which distressed managers two main approaches to investing in distressed securities, passive and proactive, exist. (See Figure 7.6.)

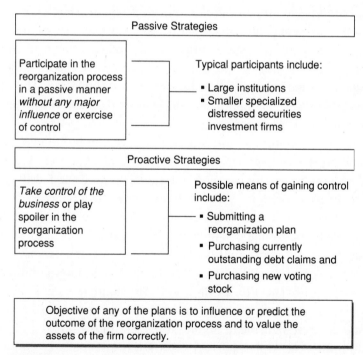

FIGURE 7.6 Distressed Investing: Two Broad Substrategies.

Passive investors are those managers who simply purchase distressed securities in the expectation that the reorganization plan carried out by others will be successful and thus result in the appreciation of the securities owned. Holders of passive strategy investments include large institutions as well as smaller, specialized distressed securities investment firms. Although opportunities for excess returns from passive strategies have been reduced by the growth in the number of market participants, the increased supply of distressed claims still makes a passive approach viable.

Proactive strategies entail varying levels of active involvement in the reorganization process. They are more time consuming, labor intensive, and costly to implement than passive strategies. Investment managers utilizing proactive strategies must, therefore, selectively limit the focus of their efforts. As a result, managers that engage in proactive strategies will tend to have a more concentrated portfolio that embodies a greater amount of unsystematic risk. These types of managers frequently have in-house legal teams to fight for advantageous treatment of their class.

Approximately 90 percent of companies experiencing financial distress will try to restructure their debt before resorting to filing for bankruptcy, and 50 percent of such companies will reach such an agreement. Out-of-court restructurings are attractive to companies because they are less expensive and pose less of a distraction than litigation. The equity markets also value this approach and historically have rewarded successful out-of-court restructurings.

Filing for Chapter 11 bankruptcy, however, can be beneficial for a company experiencing severe financial distress. Under Chapter 11, the firm does not have to pay or accrue interest on its unsecured debt or the majority of its secured debt. The firm also may reject unfavorable lease terms and borrow money from creditors that are given priority over existing creditors. Unlike out-of-court settlements, Chapter 11 reorganizations also can be accomplished without the unanimous approval of creditors. A prepackaged Chapter 11 filing represents a combination of various approaches. In a "prepack," the company simultaneously files for bankruptcy and presents a reorganization plan to creditors. The benefit is a faster settlement; about 25 percent of distressed companies use this approach. A plan of reorganization is essentially a proposal to refinance the firm's existing financial claims. In determining the value of a claim, claimholders must consider both the absolute and the relative reparation they are to receive under the proposed plan.

Proactive investors seek to profit either by redirecting the flow of corporate resources to more highly valued uses or by bargaining for a larger share of those resources by taking control of the business or by playing the role of spoiler in the reorganization process. Three possible means of gaining control are:

1. A reorganization plan can be submitted by either current management or company claimholders. The plan specifies the manner in which the firm's assets will be divided among the claimants and therefore can be written to favor one class of holders over another. Multiple plans can be submitted and voted on to determine the final reorganization plan.
2. Outstanding debt claims often are purchased with the anticipation that they will be converted into voting stock. When purchased in sufficient quantity, this action can give control to the holders of the firm's assets after reorganization.
3. The purchase of new voting stock, referred to as funding the plan, can give buyers control of the company and its assets, if they purchase sufficient shares.

The purchase of currently outstanding equity prior to reorganization is rarely an attractive option because of the dilution that occurs as a result of any reorganization. The keys to any of these three strategies are to influence or predict the outcome of the reorganization process and value the firm's assets correctly.

Control also can be exercised by establishing a blocking position in any of the classes of claims. This strategy, called bond mail, involves playing the spoiler by delaying approval of the reorganization plan. Under Chapter 11, each class votes separately on whether to approve the consensual reorganization plan under consideration. Approval by a class of claimholders requires acceptance either by a two-thirds majority in value or by one-half in number. By purchasing slightly more than one-third of the value of claims in a single class, one investor sometimes can block the reorganization plans in the hope of gaining a concession for the entire class. The ability to carry out this strategy effectively depends on both the structure of the classes and the number and makeup of claimholders. The reorganization plan can, however, sometimes be crammed down (approved despite the objections of a single class).

The role of distressed investors (or vulture investors) in corporate reorganizations is controversial. In the long run, if the distressed investors are deemed to be detracting value from the process, they will be shut out. Many bankruptcy judges are philosophically opposed to the idea that people can insert themselves into a distressed situation for profit while the firm's original lenders and stockholders are being asked to make material financial sacrifices. Such hostility, however, overlooks the critical role that investors play in creating value in a restructuring situation. A key point to consider is that trading in distressed claims is voluntary. Sellers participate in a given transaction only when they expect to benefit from doing so. There exist numerous situations in which original lenders can benefit from selling their claims. Furthermore, by buying and consolidating claims, distressed securities investors can expedite the reorganization process by reducing holdouts and by having the flexibility to enter the reorganization process from the point of view of discount buyers.

Some distressed securities managers also invest in equity securities that are issued at the end of the bankruptcy proceedings. These securities, called stub equities, often are overlooked by traditional investment managers. Other distressed securities funds have moved into the loan origination business. These managers have a more creative approach to the market than traditional lenders and are willing to do the work to accurately appraise unusual types of collateral. The loans are typically short term, highly collateralized, and very expensive. Lending rates typically start at 15 percent. Although commonly viewed as a risky investment, volatility in stub equities actually varies with the strategies employed and the securities held. Volatility of returns is greatest among those managers investing in high-yield debt and postbankruptcy stub equities. Lower-volatility investments include late-stage investing in senior secured debt. Financial leverage typically is not employed in this strategy.

The strategies for investing in distressed debt are many and varied. However, investors who are consistently successful in this market tend to exhibit superior skills in certain key areas:

- Valuing assets, including locating, collecting, and analyzing information
- Negotiating and bargaining
- Understanding the firm's capital structure as well as the legal rights and financial interests of all other claimholders
- Risk management, including a thorough understanding of the specific risks associated with investing in distressed situations

The level of supply of distressed paper is a key determinant of profitability in this strategy, as the level of pricing is determined by the supply of investment opportunities in the market. As mentioned earlier, investment in this strategy entails the purchase or sale of securities at different levels of the capital structure. As the supply of such securities increases in the market, market dynamics force prices to be depressed, allowing distressed investors to purchase these securities at deeper discounts.

The level of demand for distressed securities is also a key determinant of profitability. Along with supply, demand plays a pivotal role in determining pricing. Demand typically increases when distressed investors become more active in the strategy due to the level of opportunities within the strategy. As the level of demand increases, there is less pricing pressure, which allows credit spreads to tighten.

The rate of defaults is probably the most important driver, as it has a direct impact on the supply of distressed investment opportunities in the market. The default rate is driven by many factors, including the state of the economy and credit markets in general. As the economy enters a period of recession, companies become more prone to reductions in revenues and earnings. Providers of credit then become more reluctant to provide credit, leaving companies unable to refinance existing debt or finance business operations. Conversely, as the economy improves, fewer companies default, reducing the overall supply of distressed situations.

One key strategy risk is the state of the economy. This strategy benefits from a downturn in the economy, as more investment opportunities become available in such a market environment. However, if the economic downturn is prolonged, then the recovery of these companies may be protracted or put at risk. An improvement in operating performance is contingent not only on an issuer's ability to raise cash,

Distressed investing provides factor-specific exposure,
with moderate equity market beta.

Strategy Intention	• Generate profits from securities undervalued relative to both the economic value of the firm and the projected value of the firm's other debt instruments
Source of Profits	• Buying cheap prior to restructuring "exit catalysts" • Regulatory arbitrage
Risk Return Profile	• High alpha (verses equity indices) • Moderate beta (generates returns with long bias and some downside risk) • High returns with medium risk
Role in Portfolio	• Factor-specific exposure • Long bias • Average year: 18.07% Worst year: 1998 (−4.23%)
Risk Exposure	• **Interest rate risk:** moderate • **Funding liquidity risk:** high • **Equity market risk:** high • **Leverage risk:** moderate • **Credit risk:** high • **Operational risk:** moderate • **Counterparty risk:** high
Scenario Factors	**Worst-Case Factors:** **Favorable:** • Widening credit spreads • Years following recession • Recessionary years • Equity-friendly environments • Restricted capital markets • Significant supply of distressed debt

FIGURE 7.7   Distressed Investing Strategy Profile.

deleverage, and restructure but also depends on currency, interest rates, and commodity price movements.

Distressed managers also face the risk of fraud. Thorough due diligence and risk management procedures will help protect their investments, but risk can never be eliminated entirely. (See Figure 7.7.)

Another risk is that companies cannot navigate the corporate restructuring process successfully and that certain securities do not perform as anticipated at the conclusion of the reorganization. A number of people, including bondholders, bankers, equity holders, lawyers, and judges, are involved as each company works through the restructuring process. As a result, it can be difficult to determine which group of investors will come out on top. However, in the United States, bankruptcy laws are in place to give investors a fairly good sense of the probabilities for the different potential outcomes.

The 2000 to 2002 surge in distressed securities on the market created a supply/demand imbalance offering a multitude of good opportunities for investors, much like the recession-era early 1990s, which brought strong returns for distressed securities funds. (See Figure 7.8.)

By most accounts, the U.S. economy is expected to grow at around a 4 percent rate in 2004. There is strong evidence that employment is improving, and despite an expected slowdown in consumer spending, capital spending is expected to take up the slack given the improved corporate balance sheets. There are still some potential factors that could slow growth—in particular geopolitical risks or an extended decrease in consumer spending. However, despite these risks, it appears that the economic recovery will be sustained, and inflationary pressures from a falling dollar and fiscal deficits will most likely slow the Federal Reserve from its accommodating stance to tightening.

Distressed securities should have another positive year in 2004, albeit not at the rates of 2003. Due to the historic levels of corporate defaults in recent years, a large number of bankrupt companies are progressing through the restructuring process. Thus a good supply of

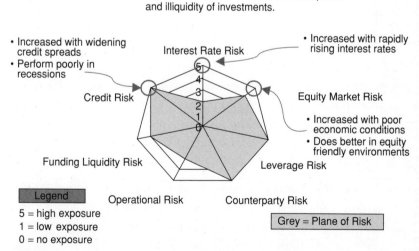

FIGURE 7.8 Distressed Investing Risk Profile.

investment opportunities in companies in late-stage bankruptcy should continue. These securities often can appreciate rapidly as the bankruptcy process approaches its resolution and the intrinsic value is realized.

Additionally, managers have noted that the move in the capital markets from traditional lenders to the less restrictive, more flexible high-yield markets may extend the distressed investing cycle. Companies rescued by the available financing that do not fix their operational problems most likely will continue to experience problems going forward.

Looking ahead, one concern for the distressed securities strategy is a tightening of the credit cycle with rising interest rates. Higher rates will increase the costs of funding and can result in some mark-to-market losses, but also may result in a repricing of some securities, resulting in lower entry points for investments.

In 2003 multistrategy managers were drawn to the distressed investing strategy to capitalize on the investment opportunities as the demand for high yield helped push returns higher. The increased number of managers investing in distressed securities may have more of an adverse effect in late 2004 as supply of distressed paper begins to diminish with the recovering economy and as interest rates begin to climb.

TIPS

Event-driven hedge funds seek to profit from occurrences that are part of the corporate life cycle, such as mergers, acquisitions, spin-offs, restructurings, and recapitalizations. Investors can bet on a corporate takeover through the risk (or merger) arbitrage strategy, for example, or can seek to profit from an investment in distressed securities. It is likely that the distressed sectors will perform well in the next few years as inflationary pressures push interest rates higher, and investment in this sector should not be overlooked.

■ Focus on experienced hedge fund managers who have been active in the event-driven strategy for at least several years and who have a proven ability to maneuver through less than favorable capital market environments.

- Risk arbitrage hedge fund managers focus on companies involved in mergers or acquisitions to take advantage of pricing inefficiencies in shares of those companies. Therefore, investors should be sure that managers are expert at analyzing deals and taking into account the possible regulatory obstacles and downside risks that could occur if a deal fails to materialize.
- Ask about the level of risk undertaken by fund managers, and recognize that some managers invest only in officially announced transactions, whereas others undertake a higher level of risk by investing in speculative positions at an earlier stage, such as in rumored deals.
- Remain cognizant of the potential for a wide variety of colliding trends, such as rising interest rates, falling currency rates, and rising energy costs, which may impact the capital markets going forward and making investment opportunities less plentiful and more difficult to identify.
- Increase your understanding of the bankruptcy process as well as the basics of fundamental analysis of distressed companies so you can do the proper due diligence on hedge fund managers in this strategy.
- Understand the role of passive versus active distressed securities investing (the latter are managers who get actively involved in the reorganization process).
- Know how to value assets, including locating, collecting, and analyzing information.
- Understand the nuances of negotiating and bargaining.
- Evaluate the firm's capital structure as well as the legal rights and financial interests of all other claimholders.
- Thoroughly understand the specific risks associated with investing in distressed situations.

CHAPTER 8

Evaluating Arbitrage and Relative Value Strategies

This chapter discusses two prominent types of nondirectional strategies, which help investors to isolate and capture as profit the difference in value between two related securities, regardless of the direction of the overall markets. Thus, the term "nondirectional" refers to the idea that each strategy in this category attempts to build on the notion that skilled managers can profit in any market conditions.

The terms "arbitrage" and "relative value" refer to the specific ways in which the three strategies considered in this chapter attempt to achieve alpha for investors. Strictly defined, "arbitrage" refers to a completely riskless trade that involves buying a security at a lower price in one market and immediately selling at a higher price in another market. In reality, such purely riskless trades do not exist, and so in actual practice the term refers to attempts to approximate such conditions through complicated arrangements of trades in different but closely related securities. The two arbitrage strategies considered in this chapter are convertible arbitrage and fixed-income arbitrage.

CONVERTIBLE ARBITRAGE HEDGE FUND INVESTING

To understand how the convertible arbitrage strategy invests and trades in convertible securities, it is helpful to review some basics related to convertible securities. A convertible bond is a straight corporate bond

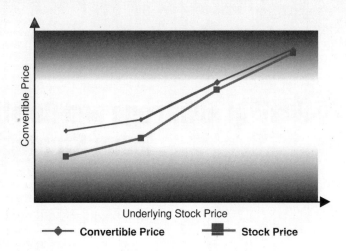

FIGURE 8.1   Convertible Bond Price Behavior.

with an option that allows the bondholder to convert to equity at predetermined periods and at a predetermined exchange rate, which is an
agreed on number of common shares, known as the conversion rate. A
convertible bond thus has certain characteristics of both a bond and
a stock. As a fixed-income instrument, a convertible bond provides
investors with downside protection in the form of guaranteed interest
payments and principal protection. At the same time, a convertible
bondholder has the opportunity to profit further if the price of the
issuer's common stock should appreciate. In terms of risk, investors who
own a convertible security are exposed to both stock market and interest rate risk. (See Figure 8.1.)

The fact that the bond is convertible into equity means that it also
includes the attributes of an option, and it is this "embedded option"
that is the source of most of the complexity of the convertible arbitrage
strategy. Like an option, after its primary issuance a convertible security
can fall into one of three states: (1) out of the money, (2) at the money,
or (3) in the money.

"Out of the money" means that the underlying stock has declined
and the conversion privilege inherent in a convertible instrument is very
little or worthless, based on the assumption that an investor is highly

unlikely to exercise the conversion option. A convertible bond significantly out of the money sometimes is referred to as a busted convertible.

"At the money" implies that the underlying stock price remains within a reasonable distance of its conversion price. Under this scenario, the convertible instrument trades at a yield advantage over the common stock, due to the downside protection offered by the convertible bond and the fact that conversion privilege has value.

"In the money" implies that the underlying stock price has risen significantly, thereby increasing the likelihood that an investor would exercise the conversion option when able to do so. The convertible bond's price behavior under this scenario is very similar to the underlying stock. As shown in Table 8.1, the rise in the price of the convertible bond reflects the upside potential available to the holder of the convertible instrument.

Convertible bond arbitrage, therefore, involves taking a long position in a convertible bond and a corresponding short position in the underlying equity, thus offsetting the risk inherent in the equity component of the bond. In this basic form, the strategy proposition is not too difficult to grasp. But, as noted, the execution of all details of even a straightforward arbitrage trade can be complicated. Generally only managers with considerable experience trading convertibles can carry out arbitrage trades. Most convertible arbitrageurs have honed and perfected their skills over many years, with the majority of them gaining

TABLE 8.1   Convertible Arbitrage Sample Deal

Company ABC Convertible Bond 7% Coupon
■ One year maturity at par of $1,000
■ Convertible into 100 shates of ABC common stock
■ ABC company common stock trading a $10 per share
■ Investment value of ABC convertible bond: $900 (based on an ABC straight bond)
■ Strategy: buy the convertible bond and short the stock with a short position of 60 shares
■ Assume short rebate rate of 60%
■ No leverage utilized for simplicity purposes

their first experience as analysts at a proprietary desk of an investment bank or a hedge fund specializing in this strategy.

Returns can be broken down into what is known as static return and dynamic return. Static return is generated by the receipt of a coupon or dividend in addition to the rebate on the short selling of the underlying stock, less any financing costs. The dynamic portion of the return is achieved when the arbitrageur hedges the position by buying or selling more or less of the underlying stock. Dynamic returns have comprised the largest portion of a convertible arbitrageur's performance over the course of several years. This is certainly the case whenever one is in a market dominated by low-coupon-paying convertibles coming to market.

Returns result from the difference between cash flows collected through coupon payments and short interest rebates and cash paid out to cover dividend payments on the short equity positions. Returns also can result from the convergence of valuations between the two securities. Risk originates from the widening of the valuation spreads due to rising interest rates or changes in investor preference.

To evaluate their performance, it is important not to lump all convertible arbitrageurs into one category, as the strategy can be implemented in many ways. For instance, many arbitrageurs prefer to focus their activities on nondistressed or nonbusted securities; others are more inclined to assume the higher risks associated with investing in busted convertible securities. Still others prefer to extract the majority of the performance from carry (static returns), while some rely less on the coupon and rebate, attempting to extract value from volatility trading (dynamic return). Generally speaking, performance attributions of convertible arbitrageurs reveal a wide mix of combinations of static and dynamic returns, as well as variation according the prevailing economic conditions of any given period. For instance, in periods of higher than normal volatility and low interest rates, it is not uncommon to see a majority of return being derived from active trading. This has certainly been the case in the last couple of years, during which volatility has risen significantly and interest rates have fallen to significantly low levels.

Although convertible securities have been around since the late 1800s, the last several years have seen several developments worth commenting on here.

Most convertible activity has taken place in the United States, Europe, and Japan, although Asia beyond Japan—particularly Taiwan, Hong Kong, and Korea—is becoming an active region for convertibles issuance. Historically Japan has represented the largest single market in terms of convertibles securities issuance. Recently, however, there has been a marked decrease in primary issuance of convertible securities there, while there has been a surge in the number of new convertible issuance in Europe and the United States. Restructuring in Europe has contributed to the growth in that region. The United States saw new issuance increase due to a large number of traditional industries utilizing the asset class as a means of finance for the first time. In addition, the fact that the initial public offering (IPO) market has not been very welcoming for the last several years has led to many corporations opting to issue convertibles instead.

The end of the long bull market also brought changes in the composition of the industries represented in the universe. Today there are fewer technology and telecom issuers in the convertibles marketplace, a far different scenario from just a couple years ago. Although both technology and telecom sectors continue to be well represented, their numbers of new issues have dwindled considerably, allowing other sectors to catch up. Much of the issuance by the technology and telecom sectors was not of the highest quality and, in fact, carried considerable risk because the majority of these issuers were companies in their infancy. Recently there has been a clear shift in the profile of the U.S. convertibles universe from that of speculative high-yield to more large-cap, investment grade issuers. Today the list of convertible issuers includes Ford Motor Company, General Motors, and Washington Mutual, to name just a few. Not only is the list broader now in terms of industries represented, the size of new issuance has increased quite significantly; recent examples are the $5 billion convertible preferred issued by Ford Motor Company in January 2002 and the $3.3 billion issuance by General Motors the following month.

European convertibles traditionally have been associated with higher credit quality, and so the significant increase in credit quality is less applicable to Europe than it is to the United States, where investors have had to work with subpar quality. Despite the drop in the number and amount of convertible issuance in Japan, Japanese convertibles were considered to be of fairly good credit and not so much of the weaker quality associated with the high-tech issues of the United States in the late 1990s. Although for most investors there has been little to do in Japan recently, some arbitrageurs continue to seek to capitalize on volatility plays, considering that static returns are at a minimum due to the low coupon rates characteristic of Japan.

Investors in convertible arbitrage strategies have seen a relatively recent growth of asset swaps and credit default swaps, which has enabled them to obtain credit protection at an affordable rate. This protection allows convertible investors to shift credit risk to investors who better understand credit and are more willing to assume this risk, while the convertible investor can focus on the equity component of the security. While asset swaps and credit default swaps are both classified as credit derivatives, there are distinct differences between the two. In an asset swap transaction, there is a transfer of physical ownership of the bonds, whereby the convertible arbitrageur sells the bonds to an intermediary (usually an investment bank) for the bond floor, yet retains the right to call the bond back in the future. A recall spread is agreed on at the initial stage of the transaction, and this spread is used should the arbitrageur wish to recall the bond. An asset swap transaction allows the arbitrageur an option on both the credit spread of the issuer and the underlying equity. In addition to the convertible arbitrageur and the intermediary, there is another party to the transaction in an asset swap: the credit investor who transacts with the intermediary. The credit investor basically buys the convertible security at par, delivers the coupons on the security back to the intermediary, and typically receives London Interbank Offering Rate (LIBOR) plus a credit spread on a periodic basis.

Credit default swaps do not entail the transfer of physical ownership of securities. Instead, convertible arbitrageurs are typically buyers of credit default protection, whereas the counterparty is the credit investor who is a seller of the credit protection. As such, the arbitrageur pays a fixed periodic payment to the seller, and in the event of a default, the seller is obligated to make the buyer whole.

The market for both credit default swaps and asset swaps has grown tremendously in the last several years, providing needed protection to those seeking it, while at the same time allowing the investor who is willing to assume credit risk the opportunity to profit from it. Now credit risk can be shifted away to a large extent, albeit at a cost, thereby allowing the convertible arbitrageur to concentrate on what he or she knows best. Regardless of the type of derivatives used, however, there is a cost involved to the buyer of credit protection. Thus, only rarely does an arbitrageur hedge all credit risk, because the additional cost can adversely affect performance. Generally, arbitrageurs are selective in their credit hedging practice; they are unlikely to hedge credit risk for issuers on whom they have conducted extensive credit analysis and thereby have attained a significant understanding of the credit risk involved. In hedging away credit risk, a buyer of protection is assuming counterparty risk, in spite of the fact that most intermediaries tend to be large financial institutions. Nonetheless, the skill required to hedge away some risk has been a positive step for the convertible arbitrage strategy. Barring any unforeseen counterparty blow-up, this ability should continue to be a positive for the strategy for the foreseeable future.

Convertible strategies perform best in an environment of declining interest rates and highly volatile equity markets. It is no secret that we are currently heading away from such an environment, as interest rates have been at historic lows for some time and are likely to be north of where they have been recently. In addition, volatility has been unusually subdued by some measures throughout long stretches in recent years.

The above points are general drivers of risk and return for this strategy. A much more specific risk to the performance of convertible arbitrageurs that is worth exploring in detail has to do with the nature of hedge fund participation in the convertibles marketplace.

Investors in this asset class can be broken down into two broad categories, outright investors and hedge fund investors. Outright investors are buyers and sellers of convertibles in much the same way that long-only buyers of common stock are, in that they are evaluating the securities on a long-only basis. Convertible arbitrageurs are using various other parameters to evaluate the value of certain securities, including but not limited to the benefits from volatility trading. A security that seems attractive to one group of investors may not necessarily be as attractive or valuable to another group; this fact can create potential investment opportunities for each group at different times. Demand from hedge fund arbitrageurs relative to demand from outright investors has been a significant factor in the rapid growth in convertibles issuance as arbitrageurs participate in the market oftentimes when outright investors are unwilling to do so. In fact, it has been suggested that current market conditions are such that many investment banks will speak with hedge fund managers prior to pricing new convertible issues in order to better understand hedge fund demand for products.

On the whole, this broader investor base and increased demand for convertible securities is positive. However, there is reason to be concerned about the impact on pricing if the recently increased hedge fund participation is ever to be significantly reduced. In other words, who will be the buyers when hedge funds become sellers, and at what price level? Without a crystal ball, it is hard to determine a price level in such a scenario, considering that there are so many other factors at work.

Although a concern for some, for others increased hedge fund participation can be interpreted as positive. In brief, this is because most hedge funds that specialize in convertible arbitrage are more than likely to remain invested in the strategy. One consequence of investor lock-up periods, not only for convertible arbitrageurs but across the range of hedge fund strategies, is that there is limited pressure from hedge fund investors to sell at the least opportune time. Thus in most cases hedge fund arbitrageurs sell only when they deem it appropriate to do so and not because of capital redemption requests caused by investor capital outflows. This flexibility can be very powerful for the strategy. In certain periods it can add stability to a strategy that previously was dominated by long-only investors who generally lacked such discipline or capital outflow controls. This is not to imply that hedge funds will not sell if markets get rough, only that they are less likely to be forced to liquidate and are able to bear temporary fluctuations a little better.

Also, hedge funds vary the level of leverage utilized and the level of cash position maintained within the fund, depending on the opportunity set. This is where a marked upswing in performance can be observed, both of individual funds and/or of the sector overall. In recent years it has become common to see convertible arbitrage hedge funds at an average leverage level of approximately 2.5 to 3.5 times, compared to average levels of approximately 5 to 7 times just a year or two earlier. This leverage level should not be construed as bearish on the strategy, but more as a reaction to changing market climates and a reflection of a more cautious risk appetite. Although the growth in new issuance has been significant and potentially a concern for some investors, concomitantly it is precisely this growth that has expanded the draw of the asset class to a broader group of investors.

The decline in volatility is indeed a valid concern. In combination with rising interest rates, it likely will impact the strategy more than any other concern. For several years, we have seen moderate returns from the strategy as compared to some stellar returns for several years earlier. There is little doubt that reduced volatility is the culprit. Compared to the broader markets, however, the strategy has outperformed quite well in spite of reduced returns. Nevertheless, most hedge fund investors are seeking absolute returns. Thus, an argument for the strategy on the basis of relative return versus broader market benchmarks can go only so far.

The outlook for convertible arbitrage in the intermediate term is positive and little changed from recent years. However, trying times lie ahead. Interest rates will rise in 2004 with the bulk of central banks' rate tightening likely occurring in 2005. Spreads also will widen, putting pressure on any management style relying on credit-sensitive convertibles to generate returns. Losses may be mitigated by the availability of instruments to hedge credit risk, such as convertible asset swaps and credit default swaps, or by instruments to hedge interest rate risks, such as interest rate futures, forwards, and swaps. However, a drawback of credit hedges is that they can become very expensive when there is heavy demand for protection. Consider these two cases.

Interest Rates Are Low and Real Rates Are Negative

We have a Federal Reserve funds rate at around 1 percent in a U.S. economy with the Consumer Price Index (CPI) and Purchasing Power Index (PPI) running at an annual rate of around 3 percent and with nominal gross domestic product (GDP) running between an estimated 5 to 6 percent. With the output gap further estimated to be 0.50 percent, higher expected growth and the improved productivity of the U.S. economy, real rates should be higher instead of their current rate of –2 percent. It is estimated that the neutral Federal Reserve funds target rate should be closer to 4 percent. The "easy money" policy is not the only stimulus propping the U.S. economy. Federal tax cuts mandated by the Bush administration tax plan, accelerated depreciated provisions on capital expenditures due to take effect this spring, and the currently depreciating dollar will only give more traction to the U.S. economy. All these monetary and fiscal policy measures amount to an enormous stimulus.

With gold's impressive performance in 2003, and continuing in 2004 with copper and oil up around 45 percent, deflation is dead and inflationary pressures are bound to build along with further moves in commodities. While Fed officials have indicated their willingness to hold rates steady, negative real rates cannot last forever in the face of widening fiscal and trade deficits. The balance of risks clearly points to upside in U.S. yields across the entire maturity spectrum and to a classical flattening of the U.S. yield curve. Not all is great in the U.S. economy, however. Consumer debt, both secured and unsecured, now represents 82 percent of GDP. This level is considered excessive by many economists, and there are fears that rate hikes will increase the burden of already leveraged consumers, causing consumer spending to decline. Because of debt fears, the absence of material inflationary pressures, the U.S. industry operating at only 75.7 percent of capacity as of November 2003, and disappointing payroll growth, we believe that the Federal Reserve is more likely to hike rates only later in 2004 with the brunt of the tightening cycle falling in 2005, when the global recovery will have taken a firm hold.

Although Japan is also experiencing a robust economic recovery led by strong exports and vigorous capital spending, its Central Bank is committed to a zero interest rate policy until it creates moderate inflation. We believe that the Bank of Japan will stick with this policy for the foreseeable future. With the increased issuance of Japanese Government Bonds (JGBs), we believe that the balance of risks in Japan points to upside in long-term yields allowing the Japanese yield curve to become steeper.

Credit Spreads Are Already Tight

There is no denying that credit spreads became tight at the end of 2003. Some managers, such as Helix Investments Partners, LLC, now believe that U.S. corporate credit spreads have reached bubble level. They note these factors:

- The average price of a high-yield bond is near $110.
- The average yield for 10-year maturities is approximately 7 percent.
- The average spread to 10-year Treasuries is approximately 250 basis points.
- More than half of the market trades above call and at an average of about 5 points.
- Approximately 80 percent of the market trades above par.
- Although spreads are still wider than their levels at a similar stage after the recession of the early 1990s, these are characteristics of a market whose upside has become very limited. Indeed, a further decline in rates or in spreads of 100 (200) basis points will change prices by only 2.75 percent (4 percent). In contrast, an increase of 100 (200) basis points will result in a price change of −5 percent (−11 percent).

These managers further note that yield declines must be driven primarily by interest rates, given the extreme tightness of current spreads, while yield increases can be driven by either interest rates or spread widening. Recall that spreads have a directional component and a pure risk or residual component. If rates rise as expected later in 2004, spreads would likely rise. Furthermore, as suggested by Helix, at spreads of 250 basis points and an average price of 110, high-yield investors need only experience a compound default rate of 2 percent to break even with Treasuries. This is significant when one realizes that the average default rate in the last 20 years has been 5.5 percent and in 4 of those 20 years, default rates exceeded 10 percent. The balance of risks is therefore more tilted toward significant widening in spreads than toward what would at best be a limited further spread tightening.

FIXED-INCOME YIELD AND SPREAD VOLATILITIES

Despite the recent favorable trend in interest rate volatility, year 2004 is characterized by high volatility. The increasingly unsustainable low short rates, in the face of robust economic growth, will generate more volatility as the prospects of vigorous Federal Reserve rate hiking activities loom over the course of the year. The increase in volatility is likely to come from episodes of deleveraging and mortgage hedging stampedes created by sharp bond sell-offs. Furthermore, with deepening budget and trade deficits and a weakening dollar, the idiosyncratic influence of foreign entities financing U.S. deficits will contribute to the instability. To these factors should be added war, terrorism, and company/industry events. Increased volatility will likely contribute to spread widening.

EQUITY VOLATILITY: AT THE LOWER END OF ITS RANGE

As mentioned previously, equity volatility as measured by the Chicago Board of Trade volatility index trended down significantly in 2003 and is near the lower end of its range. We expect equity volatility to continue to fluctuate against the put/call ratio as the decline in equity risk premium is offset by instability created by deficits, exchange policies, the Federal Reserve's changing stance, and other factors already discussed.

NEW ISSUANCE IS KEY

As long as interest rates remain low and equity markets remain strong, a healthy new-issue calendar is expected. Note that new issue activity was also robust in January 2004 as supply still appeared to lag demand.

FIXED-INCOME ARBITRAGE STRATEGIES

Investors in fixed-income arbitrage rely on hedge fund managers who take long and short positions in bonds and other interest rate–dependent securities. Generally, a manager pursuing this strategy seeks to identify securities that approximate one another in terms of rate and maturity but for some reason are suffering from pricing inefficiencies. Risk varies dramatically from fund to fund, depending on the types of trades that are made and the level of leverage employed. Because this universe is so large and diversified, and because performance of these funds can differ appreciably, it is particularly important to understand the range of factors involved in how fund managers are attempting to achieve alpha and what risks they are willing to accept to do so. (See Table 8.2.)

TABLE 8.2 Fixed-Income Arbitrage at a Glance

Historical return	10%–12%
Historical volatility	Low (4%–5%)
Risk characteristics	Varies by strategy
Expected correlation with equity markets	Low (0.4)

Source: LJH Global Investments, LLC.

Investors are likely to see fixed-income managers experiencing volatility between 8 percent and 10 percent in the next few years, and performance will likely vary appreciably across funds. Therefore, it is particularly important to understand how fund managers are attempting to achieve alpha and what risks they are willing to accept to do so. Given the fairly conservative nature and market neutrality of most fixed-income arbitrage funds, we believe that this strategy is a good addition to a conservative, well-diversified hedge fund portfolio.

Diversified fixed-income managers who engage opportunistically in all forms of arbitrage strategies and in high-yield securities have had strong performance in recent years. Most managers were up more than 15 percent in 2004 with a few up nearly 30 percent. In contrast, yield curve arbitrage hedge funds had a positive but subdued year with significant variations across managers. Typical performance was around 4 percent among managers whom LJH tracks. Managers who performed significantly better also took more risks by engaging in arbitrage across curves and therefore exposing themselves to spread risks. In aggregate, the fixed-income arbitrage sector performed well in 2003 and continues to provide strong opportunities in 2004.

Fixed-income arbitrage can be broken down into three general categories: (1) global yield curve arbitrage, (2) mortgage arbitrage, and (3) credit arbitrage.

Global yield curve arbitrage is a diversified strategy that uses a variety of liquid and highly rated fixed-income instruments from around the world to create relative value and directional positions within a given yield curve or between different curves. These instruments may utilize or combine cash securities, swaps, swaptions, futures, and other derivatives instruments. Global yield curve strategies tend to be very liquid. (See Table 8.3.)

TABLE 8.3   Fixed-Income Substrategies

Mortgage-related Substrategies	Global Fixed-Income Substrategies
■ MBS (pass-through securities) ■ CMBS (commercial mortgage securities) ■ CMOs (MBS derivatives)	■ Yield curve ■ Relative value ■ Basis

Mortgage arbitrage invests in high-yield mortgage-backed securities, including mortgage pass-throughs, interest only (IOs), principal only (POs), floaters, inverse floaters, and planned amortization class (PAC) bonds. The strategy attempts to hedge market exposure by using Treasuries, swaps, agency debentures, and other mortgage instruments and options. Unlike most fixed-income securities, the mortgage market, and notably collateralized mortgage obligations (CMOs), are full of securities with huge variations in positive duration (POs, inverse floaters) and negative duration (IOs, floaters). Because these complex instruments yield more than the cost of short-term borrowing, hedge fund managers use leverage to create high-yield, market-neutral portfolios. To a large extent success is determined by managers' ability to model realistically and hedge the embedded options in these instruments. The liquidity of these types of funds can vary significantly, ranging from very liquid to fairly illiquid.

Credit arbitrage is a strategy that seeks to take long and short positions in high-yield corporate bonds and hedge out the noncredit exposure using Treasuries, credit default swaps, and other corporate securities such that the only exposure remaining is the underlying credit of the company. This strategy tends to be moderately liquid to fairly illiquid.

Finally, many fixed-income hedge funds are diversified and they engage opportunistically in all previous three forms of arbitrage. Also, not all of their positions are hedged to remove market exposure. Consequently, at times the portfolios may contain a significant degree of directional exposure. It is probably more appropriate to characterize such hedge fund managers as "long/short" rather than "market neutral."

There are two fundamental strategies in the fixed-income arbitrage universe: trading low-yield liquid securities and using significant leverage, or trading high-yield illiquid securities and using low to moderate leverage.

Because liquid securities tend to be lower-yielding instruments, these types of trading strategies generally depend more on asset appreciation to achieve their return objectives. The illiquid strategy, however, is typically more reliant on the "carry" of the portfolio (the yield earned on a position relative to the cost of financing the position). The key to solid performance for the fixed-income arbitrage sector is market volatility.

According to modern capital market theory, risk and return are related in equilibrium. Consequently, we can make sense of what drive returns or performance by focusing on the risk factors for the strategy. Although risk is a multidimensional concept, the performance of fixed-income arbitrage as a class is driven by the interplay of three risk factors: (1) interest rates, (2) volatility, and (3) credit spreads.

Interest Rates

Changes in interest rates represent one of the greatest risks for a fixed-income fund, as interest rates directly impact the value of most fixed-income securities. How sensitive a fund is to changes in interest rates depends on the effective duration of that portfolio. Although important, duration risk is not the only risk faced by fixed-income managers. Most fixed-income arbitrage funds try to maintain a market-neutral portfolio, which would suggest that they would not be markedly impacted by changes in interest rates. Unfortunately, duration risk is not the only source of risk fixed-income managers are exposed to. As proxies for movements in the yield curve, we may focus on changes in the 3-month U.S. Treasury bill and in the 10-year Treasury note.

Market Volatility

Changes in interest rates tend to be accompanied by changes in the volatility of rates. Changes in volatility cause a change in the curvature of yield curve (convexity risk). They affect the valuation of other fixed-income securities through the put/call options of the callable corporate bonds, of mortgage securities (e.g., prepayment risk), or of those embed-

TABLE 8.4 Fixed-Income Arbitrage
Price Volatility Drivers

- Yield curves
- Volatility curves
- Expected cash flows
- Credit ratings
- Currency valuations
- Special bond and option features

ded in spread products. Although market volatility can create trading opportunities, too much volatility creates additional risks that affect the ability of fund managers to put on and maintain effective hedges. It can cause the correlation between long positions and hedges to diverge, resulting in the appreciation of the hedge and the depreciation of the long position. (See Table 8.4.)

For example, if a fund were to have a long position in mortgage pass-throughs and were to hedge that position with U.S. Treasuries, and the markets were to become very volatile, mortgage spreads might widen due to credit concerns and at the same time Treasuries might rally as investors take a flight to quality. The result would be a loss on both sides of the trade. Most yield curve arbitrage managers generally use "butterflies" to create positions that are market neutral (i.e., immune to both parallel shifts and changes in the slope of the yield curve). However, these positions are generally ineffective against changes in the curvature of the yield curve.

In summary, hedging interest rate risk is complex and dynamic. Therefore, it is rare that a fixed-income fund portfolio remains truly market neutral in the face of sharp moves in interest rates and/or heightened volatility. Good proxies of interest rate volatility include the implied volatility of the 10-year Treasury options with 3 months to expiration and the swap volatility.

Credit Spreads

Credit spreads provide a measure of the perceived risk of investing in fixed-income securities. As an economy weakens and the credit quality of bond issuers deteriorates, investors require higher yields to compensate for the increased risk. These higher yields represent a wider spread over Treasuries and lower prices (i.e., asset depreciation).

It is important to note that credit spreads have a directional component. Some portion of the change in credit spreads depends solely on changes in Treasury rates. The residual component is a better measure of the pure risk of investing in fixed-income securities (spread risk) than the total change in spreads. Factors influencing spread risk include equity market returns and implied equity market volatility measured, for example, by the VIX index. Instead of focusing on corporate spreads to Treasuries, many investors in the fixed-income industry prefer to focus alternatively on the more generic swap spreads and on swap rates in place of Treasury rates.

Substrategies such as yield curve arbitrage are not impacted significantly by changes in credit spreads unless they take positions across different yield curves. To protect themselves, yield curve arbitrage hedge funds may carry swap spread widener trades in their books. In general, credit exposure is generally not a significant risk component. However, it is a major component of credit-risk arbitrage and high-yield hedge funds. Changes in spreads also will impact mortgage hedge funds, although to a lesser extent than the lower-rated corporate securities because the underlying mortgage pools typically are well diversified and tend to be highly rated.

Diversified fixed-income managers who engage opportunistically in all forms of arbitrage strategies and in high-yield securities had a great year. Although the Hedge Fund Research (HFR) Fixed Income Diversified Index was up 12.47 percent in 2004, the majority of the managers that we track were up more than 15 percent with a few nearly up 30 percent. In contrast, yield curve arbitrage hedge funds had a positive but subdued year with significant variations across managers. Typical performance was around 4 percent among managers that we track. Managers who performed significantly better also took more risks by engaging in arbitrage across curves and therefore exposed themselves to spread risks. In aggregate, the fixed-income arbitrage sector performed well in 2003. The HFR Fixed Income Arbitrage Index gained 9.04 percent.

A look at recent statistics sheds some light on the inner workings of the fixed-income arbitrage strategy. Although interest rates rose moderately in 2003 (+43 basis points for the 10-year U.S. Treasury), they fell substantially during the first half of the year, and 10-year U.S. rates fell by as much as 71 basis points by mid-June. Although a sharp correction in July and August saw these rates rise by 110 basis points before trending down moderately for the balance of the 2003, their low absolute levels and the Federal Reserve's readiness to hold rates steady against the backdrop of historically low inflation provided another positive backdrop. The strong rebound in equity markets (+28.68 percent for the S&P 500), dwindling equity volatility, rising corporate profits, low corporate default rates, the absence of a major corporate scandal, and very strong mutual fund inflows are some of the factors driving down the risk premium in high-yield securities and helping lift valuations in 2003. Mirroring the movements of credit spreads in 2003, the Chicago Board Options Exchange S&P volatility index which started the year at 28.62 stood at 18.31 at the close of the year.

Mortgage-backed hedge funds also had a good but not spectacular year in 2003 in what proved to be a challenging environment. The HFR Fixed Income Mortgage-Backed Index rose 6.88 percent. However, performance varied significantly across managers. Managers had to deal with the strong U.S. Treasury market rally during the first half of the year as declining rates led to pressure on mortgage spreads (in part caused by increased prepayment risk or convexity risk and new supply issues). Interest rate volatility and spread volatility, which were relatively high during the whole period relative to 2002 (war risks, terrorism risks, deflation risks, etc.), reached unprecedented levels in the third quarter. Implied volatility in options markets spiked more than 300 basis points in the face of both strong actual U.S. economic performance in the third quarter (with concurrent Treasury market sell-off of July and August) followed by increased concerns over the strength and sustainability of the newly found economic recovery (Treasury market rally in September). This unprecedented volatility made hedging of convexity risks difficult and also took a toll on the cost of hedging and significantly reduced the carry offered by mortgage securities. Implied and

TABLE 8.5 Outlook for Fixed-Income Arbitrage

Economic Environment	Investment Implications
■ Inflationary expectation declining ■ Fed lowering rates ■ Steepening U.S. yield curve (as well as some foreign yield curves)	■ Cheaper financing costs ■ Increasing risk tolerance ■ Significant new fixed-income issuance ■ Varying market outlooks for the different market participants

actual volatility started to subside in the fourth quarter, and so have mortgage prepayments.

The outlook for fixed-income arbitrage in the intermediate term is positive. However, the writing is on the wall. Interest rates have begun to rise slightly in 2004 with the bulk of central banks' rate tightening likely to occur in 2005. At that point, most fixed-income managers will have no place to hide. (See Table 8.5.)

What are the implications of these developments for the different substrategies? If the Federal Reserve hikes rates violently, as it did in 1994, then, as suggested earlier, there would be no place to hide and fixed-income managers may expect a bad year; high-yield managers would be at the most risk. However, we believe for reasons that the Federal Reserve will not be aggressive at this time. Under this scenario, we expect all substrategies to do well but nowhere near 2003 performance, especially so for high-yield managers, a substrategy that is likely to come under stress as the year progresses. With interest rate markets trading in a range in the intermediate term, mortgage-backed managers should perform just as well as in 2003 or better, being able to take advantage of trading opportunities without wild swings. Although increased short rates reduce the carry, the slowdown in mortgage prepayment speeds also will help. As the yield curve flattens later in the year, managers will get increasingly challenged. Global yield curve managers should do better than in recent years as the change in Central Bank regimes may lead to increased inconsistencies in global yield curves and therefore to increased trading opportunities. Nimble diversified fixed-income hedge funds should expect another solid year in a progressively challenging environment.

TIPS

Skilled hedge fund managers can profit under any market conditions, and investors should consider the addition of nondirectional hedge fund strategies to their portfolio. Known as arbitrage or relative value strategies, these funds help investors to isolate and capture as profit the difference in value between two related securities, regardless of the direction of the overall markets.

Convertible Bond Arbitrage
- Understand that a convertible bond allows the bondholder to convert to equity at predetermined periods and at a predetermined exchange rate, thus exemplifying characteristics of both a bond and a stock.
- Know that as a fixed-income instrument, a convertible bond provides investors with downside protection in the form of guaranteed interest payments and principal protection or the opportunity to profit if the price of the issuer's common stock should appreciate.
- Grasp the basics of convertible bond arbitrage, which are that taking a long position in a convertible bond and a corresponding short position in the underlying equity may offset the risk inherent in the equity component of the convertible bond.
- Consider that risk originates from the widening of the valuation spreads due to rising interest rates or changes in investor preference.
- Realize that some arbitrageurs focus on nondistressed or nonbusted securities, while others are more inclined to assume the higher risks associated with investing in busted convertible securities.

Fixed-Income Arbitrage
- Fixed-income arbitrage hedge fund managers take long and short positions in bonds and other interest rate-dependent securities, with various levels of risk and leverage.

- Three categories of fixed-income arbitrage are global yield curve arbitrage, mortgage arbitrage, and credit arbitrage, and the strategies' nuances should be clarified prior to making an investment.
- Evaluate the fund's level of sensitivity to changes in interest rates.
- Look into market volatility and how it can create trading opportunities, because too much volatility creates additional risks that affect the ability of fund managers to maintain effective hedges.
- Use credit spreads as a measure of the perceived risk of investing in fixed-income securities.

CHAPTER **9**

The Time Is Now for Equity Market Neutral

As is the case with convertible arbitrage and fixed-income hedge fund investing, equity market neutral is characterized as a relative value strategy. However, it is not pure arbitrage; this strategy generally trades on the differences in value across a wider range of less closely related securities, which is not the case in convertible arbitrage and fixed-income arbitrage.

Equity market-neutral managers construct portfolios that have close to equal amounts of offsetting long and short equity positions. By balancing long and short positions, market-neutral managers attempt to mitigate events that affect the valuation of the stock market as a whole, which implies very low or no correlation to the market. Investors in equity market neutral strive to generate consistent returns in both up and down markets.

To determine the right time to start ramping up the market-neutral allocation to one's investment portfolio, it is first necessary to understand what has been holding this strategy back as compared to other strategies. Examination of recent past performance might help determine when these adverse conditions have been alleviated. Investor sentiment points to the lack of market volatility as the culprit, yet this is not entirely accurate. Although volatility is indeed vital to the success of many market-neutral strategies, statistics support the fact that volatility is not the sole issue with which to be concerned. The popular VIX, Chicago

Board Options Exchange volatility index, which measures implied volatility, has been registering a comfortable mid-20s reading since 1997, which is impressive considering that a register of 20 is considered healthy volatility. This average had not been seen since the Gulf War days and suggests no lack of overall market volatility.

That index is, however, not perfect, because it measures end-of-day implied volatility; intraday volatility would provide a better sense of the opportunities available during the day. However, since it is the best measure available, it is worth analyzing in more detail. Consider a regression analysis, where the VIX Index is the independent variable and the HFR Equity Market Neutral Index over the last decade or so is the dependent variable. The correlation is around –6 percent, strongly suggesting that overall volatility should not be viewed as the primary driver of market-neutral returns. Clearly, however, low market volatility tends to decrease the number of alpha-generating opportunities available to equity market-neutral managers. When market volatility subsides, market efficiency tends to rise. As mentioned, equity market-neutral managers prefer those periods of volatility so that they can go after additional profits. (See Table 9.1.)

TABLE 9.1   CBOE Volatility Index Gauges Market Volatility

Year	VIX
1997	24.01
1998	24.42
1999	23.40
2000	26.85
2001	23.80
2002	28.62
2003	18.31

Source: Provided courtesy of Chicago Board Options Exchange, Incorporated.

The VIX Index, a key measure of market expectations of near-term volatility conveyed by S&P 500 stock index option prices, is considered by many to be the word's premier barometer of investor sentiment and market volatility.

Managers use a variety of methods to mitigate market influence on their funds. Some use pair trading, which involves purchasing one security and selling short a fundamental sibling using a preset ratio to eliminate the effects of market and sector risks. For example, if an investor bought Diamond Offshore Drilling and sold short Noble Drilling Corp., he or she would be exposed to similar risks on a market and sector basis because both companies are energy drilling ones with similar assets located in similar geographic regions. The key to success relies on determining which security to buy and which to sell. In essence, the process aims to isolate the security selection skill of portfolio managers or, in the case of technical managers, their ability to construct the appropriate models to capture the relative inefficiencies between securities. Talented managers can do this effectively and capture alpha from dynamics that may alter the spread between securities. Others add, or use exclusively: a beta-neutral strategy, where positions are taken based on a stock's level of market risk; a dollar-neutral strategy, where equal dollars are invested on both the long and short sides; mean regression, where positions are taken with the idea that the securities will revert to their historical relationships their trading relationship will hold; or numerous other combinations.

No universally accepted definition of equity market neutral exists, yet an increasing commonality among funds executing this strategy is the use of complex statistical models to capture numerous market-neutralizing dynamics.

These hedge funds can appear attractive because they are designed to make money regardless of market movement and thus tend to be safe havens for excess capital. Because the strategy is generally long and short similar equities, the absolute direction of the securities matters less than the relative movement of the securities. Provided the long outperforms the short, the strategy will make money. The strategy's return is a function of the movement of the long and short security in addition to dividends received and paid, which are added to the short sale interest.

The obvious question is how the equity market-neutral strategy has performed relative to the market. The HFR Market Neutral Index, which monitors a broad representation of equity market neutral hedge funds, has maintained a less than 15 percent correlation to the S&P 500, Dow Jones, Nasdaq, and the Morgan Stanley Capital International Europe, Australasia, Far East, which measures international equities. In addition, the Market Neutral Index has maintained a far superior risk-adjusted return to the broad market, as evidenced in a much greater Sharpe ratio.

At the most general level, return from equity market neutral is derived from three sources: profits of both long and short positions and interest from margin deposits on the short positions. More specifically, the key factors that drive returns for this strategy include market volatility, market rationality, and not-so-strong bull markets.

Market volatility is important because it allows managers to benefit from information inefficiency by capitalizing on times when certain stocks may be trading away from their fundamentals, based on something not being factored in correctly or because of numerous other events.

Market rationality is probably the most critical driver of profitability of equity market-neutral managers. The strategy profits when market perception and reality are aligned, specifically, in an environment where good earnings announcements and earnings growth lead to higher stock performance and, conversely, when no earnings or growth potential lead to lower stock performance of companies. Therefore, to market-neutral managers, security selection is a vital component of success. Equity market neutral involves trading absolute positions for relative outperformance and, as a result, which side of the trade tends to matter more than the trade itself. As a result, if the perception/reality argument is out of line, the strategy will suffer. (See Table 9.2.)

Strongly bullish markets matter in that during these times, equity market neutral will tend to underperform the market simply because

TABLE 9.2   Market-Neutral Equity at a Glance

Historical return	10%–12%
Historical volatility	Low (3%–5%)
Risk characteristics	Conservative
Expected correlation with equity markets	Low (0.1)

returns are truncated by the short security component of returns. In strongly bear markets, the strategy tends to outperform the market.

What is needed to swing the market-neutral pendulum into vogue is a realignment of reality and perception. This situation will occur when earnings and cash flow performance are reflected in the movements of security prices. During the past couple of years, attention has focused on the fact that implied valuation of the market was too high, and the debate thus was about "irrational exuberance," the need to change valuation parameters in a new economy, and, more recently, the quality of earnings. These discussions focused on broad valuation issues rather than on individual security circumstances. Even now, with the market having adjusted somewhat since the Internet years, the forward price/earnings of the S&P 500 is still over 20 times next year's earnings. This is not cheap by any stretch of the imagination, given historical standards, but is much lower than the high-flying period from late 1998 to early 2000.

More critical than forward multiples, though, is the perception versus reality argument. Specifically, the environment should show good earnings announcements and earnings growth to achieve higher stock performance. Back in the dot-com heyday, market-neutral managers found themselves laggards to their competitors because they were managing against the seemingly unreachable expectations of dot-com companies. Good news translated not only into better stock performance, but also into unjustifiable security performance. Scores of companies announced better-than-expected numbers only to see their stock plummet, while others missed their expectations and witnessed an appreciation of their security. In short, the environment was dominated by macro factors, which thus relegated individual security valuation issues to a subordinate role. Indeed, even though fund managers may have made the correct analysis on a security relative to other comparables, losses may have resulted because the market was looking past valuations. Although this example is a simple one, it highlights how good fundamental work still can lead to bad results.

Security selection risk is critical to the success of the strategy. Because of the relative return nature of the strategy, being able to choose the outperformers and underperformers is the bottom line in equity market neutral. Rational markets are vital to the strategy's success. The strong bull market of late is characterized by investors rewarding speculative lower quality stocks making it very difficult to identify short candidates. The unusual component of this market behavior was persistence, something that many market-neutral managers have not experienced in the past. (See Figure 9.1.)

The year 2003 brought another problematic year for equity market-neutral managers. The HFRI Market Neutral Index posted returns of –2.38 percent, while the S&P 500 and the Nasdaq posted returns of 28.3 percent and 50.6 percent, respectively. The strong bull market adversely affected the strategy, held back by the mandated offsetting short equity positions. The end of the war in Iraq, low interest rates, favorable tax law changes, and fiscal stimulus helped create a strong rally in the equity markets that persisted throughout the year. Investors' willingness to increase their risk tolerance helped push higher not only undervalued quality stocks, but also low-quality speculative stocks that are usually held short by market-neutral managers. Consequently, for most of the year, market-neutral managers saw the gains in their long portfolio more than offset by losses in their short portfolio. This persistence has happened only two other times since 1986. The rally in low-quality stocks was further aggravated by the "short squeeze" when managers trying to cover their short positions pushed prices even higher.

Market-neutral managers who focused on mean regression also suffered from a market where opportunities for this style of trading were minimal. Reduced market volatilities persisted for most of the year, providing very little mean reversion opportunities for statistical arbitrage market-neutral funds. The decline in volatilities was attributed to the very low level of dispersion among investors throughout the year as the equity market rallied.

The U.S. economy grew approximately 4.4 percent in the first quarter of 2004. There is strong evidence that employment is improving, and despite an expected slowdown in consumer spending, capital spending is expected to take up the slack given the improvement in corporate balance sheets. Some potential factors could slow growth, in particular geopolitical risks or an extended pause in consumer spending. However, despite these risks, it appears that the economic recovery will be sus-

Equity market neutral is a volatility reduction strategy, with very low equity market beta.

Strategy Intention	• Generate profits by taking offsetting long and short positions in related equity securities
Source of Profits	• Difference between the long and short positions • Conversion on violations of the "law of one price"
Risk Return Profile	• Purest form of alpha (verses equity indices) • Low beta (generates returns with negligible exposure to market as a whole) • Sustainable, smooth, positive returns
Role in Portfolio	• Volatility reduction • Portable alpha in fund of funds • Average year: 10.23% Worst year: 2002 0.98%
Risk Exposure	• Interest rate risk: low • Funding liquidity risk: moderate • Equity market risk: moderate • Leverage risk: low • Credit risk: low • Operational risk: moderate • Counterparty risk: low
Scenario Factors	***Worst Case Factors:*** ***Favorable:*** • Strongly bull markets • Volatile markets • Low volatility markets • Information inefficiency • High intraday volatility • Rationally driven market

FIGURE 9.1 Equity Market-Neutral Strategy Profile.

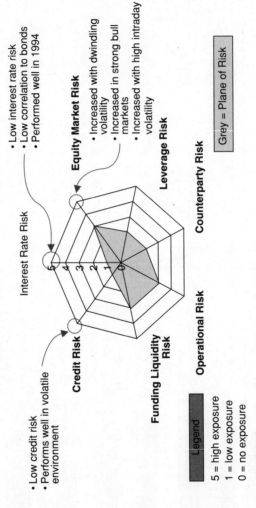

The dominant risk in equity market neutral is stock- and manager-specific, both diversifiable.

- Low interest rate risk
- Low correlation to bonds
- Performed well in 1994

Equity Market Risk

- Increased with dwindling volatility
- Increased in strong bull markets
- Increased with high intraday volatility

Interest Rate Risk

Leverage Risk

Counterparty Risk

- Low credit risk
- Performs well in volatile environment

Credit Risk

Funding Liquidity Risk

Operational Risk

Grey = Plane of Risk

Legend

5 = high exposure
1 = low exposure
0 = no exposure

FIGURE 9.2 Equity Market-Neutral Risk Profile.

Source: LJH Global Investments, LLC.

tained throughout the balance of 2004, and additional inflationary pressures from a falling dollar and fiscal deficits will most likely not push the Federal Reserve from its accommodating stance to tightening until later in 2004.

Investors will likely see a continuation of gains in the equity markets as favorable conditions accommodating fiscal and monetary policy and positive gross domestic product growth continue. Corporations look better positioned through recapitalization and reorganization; however, their equities are less undervalued than in 2003. As a result, investors most likely will focus more on fundamentals, such as earnings growth, than speculation. The undervaluation of the market has been mostly eliminated, making opportunities from risky assets less prevalent. This fact should help market-neutral managers to minimize some of the losses in their short portfolio, allowing them to refocus on their analysis and security selection skills. (See Figure 9.2.)

Inflationary pressures from commodity prices, a growing deficit, and falling currency will most likely push interest rates higher late into the second half of 2004, putting the brakes on equities and increasing volatility. Statistical arbitrage market-neutral managers who benefit from increased volatility should find the environment more favorable especially in the latter part of 2004.

TIPS

Equity market neutral is a relative value strategy that trades on the differences in value across a wider range of less closely related securities. Market-neutral managers attempt to mitigate events that affect the valuation of the stock market as a whole by balancing long and short positions. Because an investment in equity market-neutral hedge funds strives to generate consistent returns in both up and down markets, it can be a wise strategy in either an up or a down market.

- Pay close attention to the popular VIX (CBOE Market Volatility) Index, which measures implied volatility, and track how when market volatility subsides, market efficiency tends to rise.
- Know that equity market-neutral managers prefer volatile market periods when they can attempt to realize additional profits.
- Understand that other key factors that drive returns for equity market-neutral hedge funds are market rationality and not-so-strong bull markets.
- Evaluate how equity market-neutral hedge funds mitigate market influence on their funds through pair trading, beta-neutral strategies, and so on.
- Be cognizant that strategy returns are a function of the movement of the long and short securities as well as to dividends that are added to the short sale interest.
- Monitor security selection risk, which is critical to the success of the strategy; because of the strategy's relative return nature, being able to choose the outperformers and underperformers is the bottom line in equity market neutral.
- Realize that strong bull markets adversely affect the equity-market-neutral strategy, which is held back by mandated offsetting short equity positions.
- Understand that market neutral managers who focus on mean regression suffer in a market where opportunities for this style of trading are minimal.
- Corporations now appear well positioned through recapitalization and reorganization, and investors are likely to focus more on fundamentals, such as earnings growth, rather than speculation.
- Inflationary pressures from commodity prices, a growing deficit, and falling currency will most likely push interest rates higher late into the second half of 2004, putting the brakes on equities and increasing volatility.

CHAPTER 10

Long-Short Strategies in the Technology Sector

T his chapter examines how investors can take advantage of the opportunity to profit from hedge fund investing in the technology sector. Over the years, technology-focused hedge funds have turned in outstanding performance numbers while minimizing risk in the most volatile segment of the market. Investors new to technology-based hedge funds have their pick of directional or opportunistic funds. In other words, the specific investments and trading strategies are highly dependent on specific market conditions and opportunities.

The advantages of taking a long-short or hedged approach to investing in the highly dynamic, volatile technology sector are compelling. (See Table 10.1.) It is important to recognize the pervasiveness of information technology (IT) in daily life. Without our vast array of connected electronic devices, many aspects of the global economy and daily life would be inconceivable. The awareness of this reality was a significant driver of the technology bubble of the late 1990s. The Nasdaq composite index, the barometer of tech stocks, enjoyed an unparalleled run until March 2000 that created more new wealth than at any time in history. Then, just as quickly as they had gone up, the bottom fell out from under technology stocks. The highs and lows experienced by the tech market during this period in history are dramatic.

TABLE 10.1   Why Invest in a Technology Hedge Fund?

Information Technology Drivers

- Technology is key to sustain productivity increases globally.
- The Internet is changing the face of communications as well as business commerce worldwide.
- Continued convergence of technologies will accelerate the pace of economic growth and social change.
- Virtuous circle of innovation should drive new technological breakthroughs.

Medical Technology Drivers

- Aging populations in developed countries demand top flight healthcare.
- Industry consolidation improves efficiency and profitability.
- Changes to the FDA approval process as a result of the Modernization Act of 1997 may bring products to market faster and more profitably.
- Availability of genetic information; to date only 3% of human genes has been sequenced; the remaining 97% will likely be identified by 2005.
- Potential cures for certain diseases, such as cancer.

However, as demonstrated by its recent comeback beginning in 2003, and despite the devastatingly bearish years between 2000 and 2002, the technology sector still represents the most dynamic and fastest-growing segment of our economy. Companies that exploit the opportunities presented by technology have become standard-bearers for the economy overall, and the tech sector remains a leading barometer of market conditions and investor sentiment.

As the Nasdaq raced upward again in 2003, many became concerned that some of the important lessons from its late 1990s rise and subsequent crash in 2000 were too quickly or easily forgotten. Two lessons are worth noting here, principally insofar as they underscore the idea that hedged investing in the sector represents a continuously attractive option to pursue strong returns regardless of market conditions. Conversely, from a relative return perspective, overlooking these considerations will be devastating when the tech sector hits its next correction.

First, in the aftermath of the tech bubble, the notion that there are two economies at work, an old and a new, was laid to rest. Just as always has been the case, there is only one economy at work. Although the productivity improvements enabled by advancements in technology are well substantiated, the same old economic barometers of revenues and profits carry the day in the long term. The technology sector is not immune from downturns that affect the rest of the economy.

The second lesson is perhaps a little tougher to appreciate. Despite the egregious excesses of the dot-com era—a unique mixture of well-intentioned but flawed business models, speculative mania, and outright charlatanry—the simple fact is that the process of technological advancement naturally creates winners and losers, allowing the hedged investor with stock-picking prowess the opportunity to profit on both sides. Despite the fact that many investors should have known better than to buy shares in companies with neither revenues nor profits, other failed companies in the tech world are simply the makers of subpar products that cannot compete against the products of their rivals who have a marginal competitive advantage. Businesses constantly are looking for systems that will allow them to serve their customers' needs most efficiently, and technology companies that cannot consistently deliver leading products are doomed to failure. However, this continual race for the latest and greatest IT products is a positive for investors and the technology industry because it means that the industry should see greater long-term growth than other sectors of the economy. Thus, technology-focused alternative investments with a long-short strategy are an attractive way to capture the opportunities that stem from active management/absolute return strategies. Hedged investing in technology potentially offers the highest returns in the global equities markets.

Technology securities represent one of the most attractive sector plays for investors today. The sector enjoys prominence as a leader in the economy and market overall, and it is now accepted that tech valuations are not qualitatively different from other securities. Investors benefit from the high degree of competitiveness in the tech sector, which means that participants in the technology market include nearly every player in the investment world, from individual investors and money managers to institutions, venture capitalists, and hedge funds. The hedge fund manager relies on internally developed fundamental research, access to company management, Wall Street analysis inaccessible to the vast majority of investors, and extensive industry know-how to maximize risk-adjusted returns. Most of the strategies employed rely on buying long, selling short, and using derivatives on technology securities. Certain investments result in the manager holding significant quantities of a firm's outstanding common stock. It is interesting to compare the returns of technology hedge funds to the returns of the Nasdaq and all hedge funds.

Technology hedge funds have consistently produced strong returns while minimizing downside risk. Tech hedge funds did experience a down year in 2000 when the Nasdaq was down almost 40 percent, however, and it is evident that the ability of tech hedge fund managers allows them to maximize returns, especially on a risk-adjusted basis. The potential for superior risk-adjusted returns in technology-focused hedge funds offers performance-enhancing opportunities for investors within a well-constructed portfolio. This fact becomes more evident when comparing the average annual return and standard deviation of tech hedge funds to the Nasdaq and all other hedge funds. Not only do tech hedge funds typically have a higher average annual return than the Nasdaq, but they also have a much lower standard deviation. (See Figure 10.1.)

Technology stocks typically have traded at a premium to other sectors in terms of traditional financial ratio analysis due in large part to their prominence in the financial markets and their disproportionate potential for success in the future. Some technology companies have succeeded in justifying such rich valuations, while many others have failed miserably. Few would question that IT bellwethers Microsoft, Cisco Systems, and Intel helped define the performance of the U.S. stock market in the 1990s. Technology hedge fund strategies strive to be on the positive side of such outstanding gains, and the search for the next Intel, Microsoft, or latest innovation serves as a driving force for technology

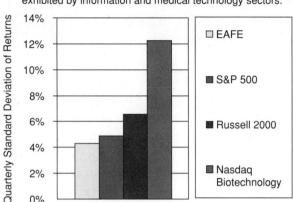

Hedged trading strategies can benefit from high level of volatility exhibited by information and medical technology sectors.

FIGURE 10.1 Inherent Volatility of Technology Sectors.

The indices are unmanaged and include reinvestment of dividends. Individuals cannot invest directly in any index. The EAFE index is an unmanaged index that is generally considered representative of stocks issued by firms in developed non-U.S. markets. The S&P 500 is an unmanaged index that is generally considered representative of the U.S. large-cap stock market. The Russell 2000 is a popular measure of the performance of U.S. small-cap companies. The Nasdaq Biotechnology is a market capitalization weight index of all Nasdaq listed stocks in the biotechnology sector.

investors. Hedge fund managers are particularly in tune to this quest and will be on the forefront of benefiting from the rapid transitions and seemingly overnight emergence of various technologies. Many investors in recent years bet on the wrong technologies or companies when picking stocks.

Also working to the advantage of hedge fund managers is the increased volatility that generally characterizes tech stocks. Hedge fund managers are better positioned to succeed in a volatile environment than other market participants due to their use of derivatives and short selling. The ability to capture value on both the upside and downside of changes in technology sets hedged managers apart from their long-only counterparts.

The risks to investors in technology companies are generally the flip-side of the advantages just outlined. The central driver of risk in technology investing is the pace at which the industry experiences change. Fortunes in the technology sector can turn dramatically, and today's high flyers may be tomorrow's dinosaurs. One element of the rate of change in technology is short product cycles, which are a major source of anxiety for IT companies. Today's cutting-edge innovation may soon be rendered obsolete by an entirely new set of technologies or a substantial improvement of an existing technology. Companies rarely bring a new product online at full efficiency; learning curves and economies of scale are captured after a sufficient ramp-up period. Technology firms must combine proficiency in new product development with excellence in manufacturing to maintain an edge over the competition.

Product cycle transitions are closely related to product cycle length. Some buyers of technology products are unwilling to spend on existing offerings and postpone purchasing decisions until a new product is released. When delays in new product introductions occur, the potential for negative near-term results can send stock prices reeling. Technology corporations must tread a fine line between milking a cash cow and delivering the latest products that customers demand.

Seasonality is another factor that typically has affected stock performance. Business in the IT industry often softens each summer, so the likelihood of earnings shortfalls is heightened during this period. Many hedge funds increase their short exposure during this period to soften the blow from disappointing earnings. One other issue that affects risk is a shortage of capable management, which afflicts many industries. The IT business is especially prone to a dearth of quality managers due to its technical complexity, frenzied pace, and minefield-laden competitive environment. Many entrepreneurs who start technology companies have no experience at managing people. Most have in-depth technical expertise but may not have the capability to grow the business without outside assistance. Managers with proven track records are valuable commodities for both fledgling and established IT companies.

Although pitfalls await tech investors, hedge fund managers who use a long-short strategy are the best-suited market participants to exploit

TABLE 10.2   Opportunities in Technology Hedge Funds

- Capture secular growth of information and medical technology industries
- Enhance return by investing opportunistically across market capitalization
- Take advantage of inherent volatility through hedge fund trading strategies
- Profit from winners and losers created by technological advancements
- Mitigate risk via low "net" exposure as well as manager and sector diversification

the opportunities made available by volatility and technological change. (See Table 10.2.) Tech investors should be prepared for periods of spotty performance, but the outlook for those who have a long-term view is bright. In the long run, technology hedge funds should continue their historical performance of strong risk-adjusted returns.

TIPS

The opportunity to profit from hedge fund investing in the technology sector is the impetus for today's technology-focused hedge funds, many of which continue to be exemplary performers with the ability to minimize risk in a volatile market segment. Both directional and opportunistic funds are available to investors, and their specific trading strategies are highly dependent on specific market conditions. Clearly, the advantages of taking a long-short or hedged approach to investing in the highly dynamic, volatile technology sector are compelling.

- Monitor the Nasdaq composite index, which is the barometer of technology stocks.

- Compare the returns of technology hedge funds to the returns of the Nasdaq and all hedge funds as part of the investment decision process.
- Analyze statistics that show that the technology sector still represents the most dynamic and fastest-growing segment of the economy.
- Know that hedged investing in technology potentially offers the highest returns in the global equities markets.
- Gather as much fundamental research as possible and be sure the hedge fund manager has appropriate access to company management, Wall Street analysis, and the extensive industry know-how required to maximize risk-adjusted returns.
- Be sure the hedge fund manager takes advantage of the increased volatility that generally characterizes technology stocks.
- Monitor the technology firms' combined proficiency in new product development and excellence in manufacturing, which helps to maintain an edge over the competition.
- Evaluate the product cycle transition period and length of the product cycle, as they may impact purchasing decisions.
- Realize that seasonality typically affects stock performance and because the IT industry often softens each summer, many hedge funds increase their short exposure during this period to soften the blow from disappointing earnings.
- Understand that long-short hedge fund managers have the unique expertise required to capitalize on available opportunities generated by volatile market conditions.

CHAPTER 11

The Expansion of European Hedge Funds

Investors looking to make an allocation to a European hedge fund historically have been limited to perhaps a handful of interesting funds. During the last two to three years, however, the European hedge fund industry has grown exponentially as hundreds of new funds have opened to meet increased demand from investors seeking ways to enhance their portfolio. Europe, and in particular London, is increasingly a key location for hedge funds that focus on investments in Europe, Asia, emerging markets, and the overall global economy. Yet despite the huge growth in the European hedge fund industry, it is still small compared to its U.S. counterpart. (See Table 11.1.)

The case for allocating capital to funds focusing on European strategies is strong, given the fact that European markets are, in general, less efficient than the U.S. markets. As a result, increasing demand from European investors, and the number of talented investment professionals in

TABLE 11.1 Growth of European Hedge Fund Assets in 2003

Region	Number of New Funds	$ Assets
Europe	228	$20 billion
United States	400	$24–27 billion

Europe, there is every reason to believe that the number of European funds will increase. (See Figure 11.1.)

Investors should anticipate a robust but declining increase in the rate of growth of European strategies in the next few years. Although equity funds in Europe—both long/short and market neutral—remain the biggest single group, they no longer account for a majority of the

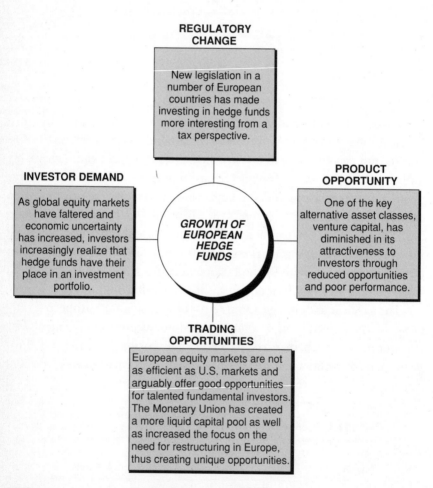

FIGURE 11.1 The European Hedge Fund Landscape.

assets. Arbitrage funds, convertible bond arbitrage; event-driven, statistical arbitrage; and quantitative strategies, have grown more strongly since 2000. Fixed-income and high-yield funds have increased most rapidly in terms of both number of funds and assets under management, but they are still underrepresented compared to the United States. Global macros also experiencing a turnaround, yet assets managed in the strategy remain status quo. Funds focusing on distressed securities and equity short sellers are few and far between.

There are a number of reasons for this growth.

- As global equity markets have faltered and economic uncertainty has increased, investors increasingly realize that hedge funds have their place in an investment portfolio.
- One of the key alternative asset classes, venture capital, has diminished in its attractiveness to investors, through reduced opportunities and poor performance.
- Investors have increasingly recognized the compelling nature of the opportunities in European markets; European equity markets are not as efficient as U.S. markets and arguably offer good opportunities for talented fundamental investors. The Monetary Union, in addition to creating a more liquid capital pool, also has increased the focus on the need for restructuring in Europe. These factors have increased interest in these markets from U.S. investors.
- New legislation in a number of European countries has made investing in hedge funds more interesting from a tax perspective.

There has been much discussion of capacity constraints among European hedge funds. The number of new funds starting up does not address this concern, because many investors will be specifically seeking funds with a reasonable track record. In a recent survey of pension funds in Europe, one of the main reasons given for not investing in hedge funds was the absence of long track records. It is true that many of the funds with long and impressive track records are closed, if not completely so, then at least to new investors. Some funds that are open to existing investors only will not be able to accept limitless amounts.

And some funds with significant assets under management probably should be closed, as they are at the point where further subscriptions could have a negative impact on returns.

These facts may appear to confirm the concern that it is difficult to get access to the best funds in Europe. However, closer inspection indicates that many of these funds actually are selectively open. Those funds that are in demand are increasingly eager to ensure a stable investor base, particularly if they offer high levels of liquidity, and therefore they leave the door open to "appropriate" investors who can demonstrate that they understand the strategy and are investing on a longer-term view.

Furthermore, the idea that only a very limited number of good managers exist in Europe is a misconception. Although some funds are constantly turning away new money and others are struggling to raise even $20 million, the levels of talent are not as unevenly distributed as these extremes may suggest. Numerous funds have strong potential and may even have developed a good track record, and they are very much open to new investors.

As discussed, the nature of most hedge fund strategies is such that there will be a limit to the level of assets under management. The potential pitfalls of having substantial assets under management have been well documented. In the same way, when looking at European funds specifically, it is necessary to look at the issues that might ensue from a fund that has a relatively small level of assets under management.

Hedge funds in Europe manage from as little as $5 million in assets up to $2.5 billion. The substantial number of new funds has meant that there are an increasing number of hedge funds managing less than $50 million in client money. On one hand, this is a positive sign, as the funds will be able to focus on the most attractive opportunities within the strategy. This fact is particularly for strategies such as merger arbitrage, in which currently very few appealing opportunities exist. Even where there is a sufficient level of good investment opportunities, smaller funds can be more flexible in approach; for example, they can take positions in smaller capitalization stocks or deals.

However, a few important issues confront smaller funds. Smaller funds may be at a disadvantage when it comes to contact with brokers and with companies; the managers may lack sufficient pull to get one-on-one meetings with company management. Investors need to bear in mind that many hedge fund managers come from backgrounds that have provided a broad and meaningful contact base and strong research capabilities. In addition, hedge funds generate considerable commissions for brokers. Their turnover levels are, on average, much higher than in a traditional fund, and it is therefore in brokers' best interests to provide a good service to the smaller funds, so as not to lose out if and when the fund grows in size.

Perhaps even more important, however, is the questionable operational viability of smaller funds. A number of funds, in some cases run by very competent managers, have closed as the revenues from management and performance fees on a relatively small asset base have not been deemed sufficient to justify continuing. The best fund managers may not be the best business managers, which funds can address by hiring someone to manage the business itself. Of course, this move means the commitment of additional resources and in most cases means releasing some equity or options over equity in the business, which in turn must be perceived as being one with good growth potential. Sometimes this can be a vicious circle. A number of larger allocators will be reluctant to invest in small funds for the reasons just discussed and also because they will not want to be holding too large a percentage of the fund. From our experience, funds tend to attract more attention from a wider range of investors when assets under management reach $50 million.

EuroHedge recently researched European hedge fund closures and particularly the main reasons behind the closures and reported that 50 of the 550 funds identified by EuroHedge as investing in European strategies have closed over the last three years. For 35 of these 50 or so liquidated funds, EuroHedge had full performance data. Of these funds, 65 percent had profitable performance, and investing in a portfolio of these extinct funds actually would have produced positive returns. These findings contradict the belief that investments in European funds bring a significantly higher risk of failure through poor performance. However, they do go some way to confirming our concern that a number of funds will close basically because they do not become profitable enough quickly enough. It should be pointed out, however, that there have been more closures since the EuroHedge article, and some were brought about by poor performance.

The size of funds can be very important in determining whether and indeed when to make an investment, particularly "boutique" hedge funds, as opposed to those managed from within a major institution. As well as ensuring that the manager has a responsible approach to asset growth, it is necessary to ensure that the manager's business at least has every chance of reaching "critical mass" in the near future and that it will be operationally viable and able to commit to adequate resources for the management of the investments and the business.

The European hedge fund industry is significantly less mature than its U.S. counterpart, and the number of hedge funds that have been in existence for more than, say, four years is small in comparison. Regardless of how impressive the manager's record is, without a track record of successfully managing a hedge fund, many investors will be reluctant to commit capital to such a fund. This is understandable, given the additional skills that are required to run a successful hedge fund, not the least of which is the ability to manage risk. In a recent example, a very successful long-only manager in Europe set up a hedge fund. The confidence in that manager was so high that large amounts of capital followed, and the new fund reached capacity in a matter of months. Such cases are, however, the exception rather than the rule.

An increasing number of firms are starting additional funds, particularly if their flagship fund is closed. If the main fund has an impressive track record and the manager is well respected, the absence of a track record for a new fund may not be considered an obstacle. But such funds should be approached with caution. In some cases, the fund may be a genuine extension of the manager's core competencies and the track record of the original fund can quite justifiably provide a historical reference for the new fund. Yet such is not always the case. Where there is an obvious diversion from the original investment strategy, the fund should be treated as any start-up fund. Often the new fund will be a multistrategy fund, and one of the substrategies will be the firm's core strategy. Due to the lower capital allocation to that particular strategy, the new fund will be able to include the best ideas from the core strategy. This is an appealing prospect, but the procedure for allocating between funds must be checked out and it must be ensured that resources, including both manpower and technology, have been suitably increased to deal with any noncore strategies. New or recent funds introduced by an established firm should be well placed from a risk management perspective; however, one of the steepest learning curves for a new hedge fund manager is often the area of risk, and having the experience with another fund should prove to be beneficial.

When evaluating funds, investors should consider firm location as part of their due diligence. Most European hedge funds are based in the United Kingdom, primarily in London. There are also funds based in the United States that operate European strategies. The importance of location depends very much on the hedge fund's strategy. It could be argued that an equity long/short fund operating in London is better placed than one based in New York, given the time difference, the proximity to the companies in which the funds are investing, and better access to market information. However, some U.S.-based funds have performed quite well, and one could argue that they have benefited from the lack of market noise that might be experienced if based in London and that they likely have a lower correlation to other funds of the same strategy. For those equity funds whose strategy is based on fundamental analysis of stocks, including meetings with managements, locations such as Edinburgh and New York will generally be adequate. The managements of most large capitalization companies are located in the cities, and London-based research analysts will visit periodically. The desire of an increasing number of investors to visit the offices of their hedge fund managers means that a particularly remote location, or one where there are hardly any other hedge funds operating, could prove to be a serious obstacle to capital raising. The impact on business risk often will outweigh the positive of a lower-cost environment.

When evaluating European hedge fund managers, it is vital to consider some of the key hedge fund strategies active in the market and how each strategy is likely to fare in the years ahead.

EQUITY LONG/SHORT AND EQUITY MARKET NEUTRAL

Equity strategies continue to dominate the European hedge fund industry, in terms of both number of funds and assets under management. Equity long/short is the main component of these funds. There are relatively few equity market-neutral funds compared to the United States, although a number have started recently to meet increased demand for such products in the current turbulent environment.

An increasing number of UK-only funds have started up. The UK equity markets are sufficiently deep and liquid that such a focus can be justified. However, the radar screen of most equity hedge funds in Europe is generally broader. These, in turn, are divided between those that take a genuinely pan-European approach and those that have a bias to a particular country or countries. Funds in which stock selection is driven by a quantitative, systematic approach are also increasing in number, but fundamental investing remains dominant. Sector funds, which focus on a particular industry, such as the technology, media, telecoms sector (TMT) or financial services, are becoming increasingly prevalent in number in Europe. Some funds manage $50 million or more, the larger funds manage in excess of $800 million.

Most European equity long/short strategies have a long bias; therefore, a key driver of performance has been and will be the performance of European equity markets. Despite the claim from most managers that their funds can produce positive returns regardless of market conditions, the performance of many equity funds was poor during 2002 and strong during 2003, indicating a relatively high correlation to the equity markets themselves. As a result, in a number of cases funds were forced to reassess their risk management, and risk overlays are being introduced and reevaluated to reduce the correlation to the market and increase the probability of generating positive absolute returns in different market conditions.

Although there are many talented stockpickers in Europe, relatively few funds actually have achieved the frequently stated aim of producing positive returns regardless of market environment; many funds with longer track records that delivered very good returns for the first two to three years have failed to do so recently, which raises concerns over their size and, perhaps more important, whether they are bull market specialists. It is likely to be awhile until the majority of investors are satisfied that there is a strong selection of effective equity long/short managers in Europe.

Shorting skills have been a subject of particular debate in the European equity long/short arena. Because hedge funds are generally new in Europe as compared to the United States, relatively fewer managers in Europe have a long track record in shorting stocks. Many managers will set up or join hedge funds directly from a traditional, long-only firm; indeed, some of the best talent from the traditional universe is being lured into hedge funds. In some cases, the manager's long-only track record has been deemed sufficient to attract vast sums of capital. It is necessary, therefore, to do an attribution analysis of a fund's returns as a means of assessing the manager's ability to short, which will not be a major concern going forward, as more and more funds are able to demonstrate a track record and allay concerns over the ability to short.

In terms of capacity, some funds manage as much as $2.5 billion in Europe-focused funds. Although the scope of a pan-European strategy is broad, this seems quite high. A more reasonable level probably is $1 billion under management. The capacity of a UK-only fund will be much lower, perhaps $300 million to $400 million, but going forward, these levels will depend on the number of funds that ultimately focus on this space. Attention also must be paid to a fund's resources to ensure that it has an adequate number of research analysts, for example, to deal with the breadth of the strategy.

A number of commentators have expressed the view that equity markets in Europe may not reach their 1999/2000 highs for as long as 15 years. This is very much a point of debate. What is not in dispute, however, is that there remains some investor uncertainty, and the prospect of continued volatility and diminished prospects for a sustained recovery in equity markets over the next 6 to 12 months. Although we continue to believe that there is a place for good European equity long/short managers in fund of hedge fund portfolios, we see the short- to medium-term outlook for equity market-neutral strategies as being more favorable.

CONVERTIBLE BOND ARBITRAGE

High-level equity market volatility is a positive for the strategy, as is a high level of new convertible issuance. In recent years, new issuance of convertibles has been high in Europe, which is a positive sign for the strategy. Although equity market volatility in Europe was very low in 2003, volatility levels going forward are difficult to predict. Volatility in credit markets and equity markets is inextricably linked. Recent new issuance of convertibles has been high in Europe, but many of these have been unattractively priced.

One of the main concerns from investors is the "crowding out" issue: A dangerously high percentage of convertible bond issues are held by arbitrageurs and imbalance will be exacerbated by the increased number of entrants into this space. Once the equity and debt markets stabilize and new issuance picks up, and assuming the continued growth of long-only convertible funds, the percentages held by arbitrageurs should be maintained at reasonable levels, particularly in large, liquid issues. In addition, the popularity of issuing convertible bonds to obtain financing means that many issues will be priced at attractive levels. Interest rate risk is another important risk for this strategy.

Clearly, the convertible bond market is constantly changing. Over the longer term, we expect the need for corporations to exploit flexibility, which is afforded by varying types of convertible structures to boost issuance once again. We believe that there will be the potential for good returns in convertible bond arbitrage in Europe.

MERGER ARBITRAGE

In the last few years there has been a considerable inflow of capital into the merger arbitrage strategy, from both hedge funds and the proprietary desks of investment banks. To meet this demand, there must be sufficient deal flow. Otherwise, if considerable capital is chasing only a few deals, spreads will narrow, thereby diminishing the attractiveness of the risk/return profile.

The level of deal flow going forward ultimately should depend on the underlying rationale/need for restructuring and consolidation in

Europe. In the short term, however, three factors will have a greater influence in determining the level of activity:

1. *Liquidity in the banking/high yield sectors:* Liquidity determines companies' ability to access debt financing.
2. *Volatility of equity markets:* Higher levels of volatility will deter potential predators from making offers.
3. *Confidence in the economic outlook:* A higher level of confidence will encourage merger and acquisition activity. (See Figure 11.2.)

A European manager will have to be familiar with the different laws and regulations governing takeover bids in the various European countries. In the United Kingdom, for example, bids cannot be made subject to financing and further due diligence as this lowers the risk of deal break, but also will generally mean lower spreads and therefore lower potential returns. The lower risk, however, will mean that managers will have a lower international rate of return threshold for UK transactions.

One of the attractions of this strategy is that the risks of positions in a portfolio will generally have a low correlation to each other, because

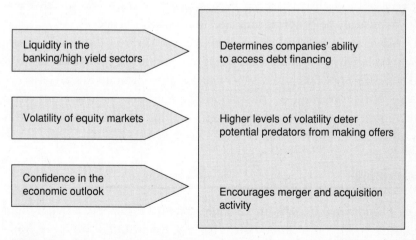

FIGURE 11.2   Factors Influencing the Level of Merger Arbitrage Activity.

the risks generally will be specific to a particular deal. Yet the terrorist attacks of 9/11 were an example of an external, systematic event that created a stronger than usual correlation between these positions.

The longer-term outlook for European risk arbitrage remains very positive, given the ongoing need for restructuring in this region. The case for consolidation in Europe is strong. European corporations are smaller and command a lower market share of their industries than their U.S. counterparts.

DISTRESSED INVESTING

Historically, the United States has been a much more lucrative hunting ground for distressed investors than Europe. However, today investors are paying more attention to Europe, essentially due to the opportunities arising from the huge increase in issuance of high-yield bonds and the high default rate (yet in nominal terms, the amounts are still much lower than in the United States). Funds are increasing their allocations to European distressed debt, and event-driven funds are increasing their allocations to distressed securities in general. A focused approach is probably preferable, as the expertise on bankruptcy law that will be required will be far more complex than for the United States alone. Also, the strategy is very labor intensive, and an experienced U.S. distressed investor will not necessarily be properly qualified to invest in Europe.

Some are concerned that the high proportion of distressed investments related to telecommunications and technology makes it difficult to comfortably value assets. However, the European distressed environment that is focusing on this is looking considerably more attractive than in recent years. Investors should note that the full potential of this strategy in Europe is yet to be seen. (See Box 11.1.)

CONCLUSION

The phenomenal growth in recent years of the European hedge fund industry is every indication that it has not reached maturity. It is, however, highly questionable whether investments in European funds will reach, even in the longer term, the same levels in absolute terms as U.S.

- We are expecting considerable fallout of hedge funds in Europe, as many hedge fund businesses become less viable due to slow asset growth and muted returns. However, we do see opportunities for strong performance.

- European equity funds have gone through a difficult time, but for the survivors we expect improved performance as risk controls have been tightened and as managers become more accustomed to shorting stock. Over the next 12 months, given the uncertain outlook for European equity markets, we would favor equity market-neutral funds over equity long/short funds.

- European convertible bond issuance reached all time highs at the end of 2001, but has since dried up as credit spreads have widened dramatically and it no longer represents a viable source of financing. However, increased volatility and the number of "cheap" convertible bonds has increased substantially, and we expect some good opportunities going forward.

- The rationale for M&A activity in Europe remains intact, but deal flow is unlikely to pick up until there is a sustained pickup in equity market valuations. Therefore, we have a negative view on European risk arbitrage in th short term.

- Although there are many distressed opportunities in Europe, these are currently too highly concentrated in TMTs to feel comfortable about backing a European only distressed fund, since the region does not in our opinion offer as attractive distressed opportunities as in the United States or Asia.

BOX 11.1 Outlook for European Hedge Funds.

funds. The investor base in Europe differs from that of the United States, as do distribution channels. Private banks are a major source of investment in Europe; broker/dealers are more prevalent in the United States. European investors appear to be more cost conscious, and the fees charged by hedge funds have been cited as a reason that many potential investors have stayed away. In addition, European investors tend to be less comfortable with the offshore structures that, in many cases, are the only means of gaining access to hedge funds.

The range of strategies offered in Europe has expanded, and this trend continues. There is no shortage of talented managers with the ability to produce excellent risk-adjusted returns, although a number have not yet developed the track records required to satisfy many savvy investors. Concerns over operational risk for smaller funds, and fewer years of experience in shorting stocks and applying sophisticated risk management techniques that are specific to hedge fund strategies, should not be ignored. Overall, however, European funds will have an increasingly important role to play in a portfolio of hedge funds. In the next couple of years there should be enough strategies and sufficient proven funds available to justify a separate European-only fund of hedge funds.

TIPS

Investors will see an increase in the number of European hedge funds in coming years. Numerous new funds are opening to meet the needs of investors who want to invest with a European-based fund and also to satisfy the demand for funds that invest in European strategies. Equity funds, both long/short and market neutral, remain the biggest single group, but no longer have the majority of European invested assets. Arbitrage funds, for example, have witnessed stronger growth over the last two to three years.

- Work with a consultant to identify the numerous funds that have strong potential, a good track record, and the capacity to take in new investment.
- Consider the issue of size versus performance prior to making an investment, because the size of European hedge funds varies from less than $5 million to $2.5 billion.
- Realize that European hedge funds have a place in an investment portfolio as global equity markets continue to fluctuate and economic uncertainty increases.

- Understand that European equity markets are not as efficient as U.S. markets.
- Evaluate new legislation in a number of European countries that has made investing in hedge funds more advantageous from a tax perspective.
- Consider the key hedge fund strategies active in the market and how each strategy is likely to fare in the years ahead.
- Study why equity strategies continue to dominate the European hedge fund industry, in terms of both number of funds and assets under management.
- Understand that the new issuance of convertibles has been high in Europe at times, which is a positive sign for the convertible bond arbitrage strategy. However, when companies are too nervous to offer convertibles, the level of issuance declines and impacts the strategy.
- Do thorough due diligence if investing in a distressed securities hedge fund since the strategy is very labor intensive and an experienced U.S. distressed investor will not necessarily be qualified to invest in Europe.

CHAPTER 12

The Dynamic World of
Asian Hedge Funds

Most investors in Asian hedge funds appear to be Americans and Europeans who seek to benefit from recent changes, such as a ruling that now allows hedge funds to be sold in Hong Kong and Singapore. Australia also is increasingly active in the hedge fund arena and represents another opportunity. Although there are signs that Asian investors are increasing their allocations to hedge funds, current hedge fund allocations are primarily to those funds focusing on U.S./European markets.

Dramatic growth in asset allocation to Asian strategies in the last several years is the result of Asian investors seeking access to absolute return strategies, of managers starting funds that focus on investing in the Asian markets, and of investors in general taking more interest in the investment opportunities available in Asia. (See Table 12.1.) As global equity markets have faltered and economic uncertainty has increased, investors have increasingly realized that hedge funds have a place in a portfolio of investments. Because the financial markets in Asia

TABLE 12.1 Growth of Asian Hedge Fund Assets in 2003

Region	Number of New Funds	$ Assets
Asia/Pacific	100	$3.7 billion
United States	400	$24–27 billion

are more inefficient than the U.S. and European markets, they arguably offer good opportunities for talented fundamental investors and arbitrageurs. Increased hedge fund education of Asian investors is also a positive for the industry.

The main source of demand from within Asia has been Japanese institutional investors. Many of Japan's most powerful institutions, including life insurers, major banking groups, trading houses, and semi-governmental lenders, have become increasingly receptive to hedge fund investment and in several cases are trying to position themselves as investors, distributors, and even managers. Japanese institutions have increased allocations to hedge funds, primarily to global fund of hedge funds, and there is some evidence that they are beginning to look more closely at domestic hedge funds.

The Japan-focused funds have benefited primarily from the actual inflow of hedge fund capital into the region. There are several reasons for this.

The boom of the 1970s and 1980s in Japan led many fund managers to build up Japanese trading and language skills to benefit from this phenomenon. Consequently the pool of talent with expertise in the Japanese markets is deeper than for the rest of Asia, which has meant an increased ability to attract capital from U.S. and European investors. Additionally, a Japan-invested hedge fund manager will claim that the Japanese stock market has the most inefficient characteristics of any of the world's leading markets. These claims have led to a myriad of opportunities for hedge fund managers on both the long and the short side of the investment spectrum. And despite the recent restrictions on shorting in Japan, it is still easier to short stock in Japan than the rest of Asia. There is a widespread belief that Japanese managers pay closer attention to risk controls and, of course, that these risks are not as difficult to navigate. Japan-only hedge funds continue to show consistent performance. (See Table 12.2.)

More than half of the assets invested in Asian hedge funds are managed from outside the region, with the main location currently being the United States. Except in Singapore and Australia, there are relatively few local managers in the Asian region. Most notably, the two most important locations for Asian-based hedge funds, Hong Kong and Japan,

TABLE 12.2 Asia Pacific: Sectors and Strategies at a Glance

- China: The growth story continues. The outlook of growth of gross domestic product and foreign direct investment into China is positive. After entering the World Trade Organization, China has been opening up more strategic industries to multinationals, and the country is now one of the most powerful manufacturing bases in the world.

- Japan: Its restructuring accelerates. The Bank of Japan initiated a buyback of a portion of equity cross-shareholdings, and the financial services authority head was reshuffled to a more reform-oriented individual. Hedge fund managers in general are positive about the events, which are expected to create more catalysts for restructurings.

- Korea: Its economy has restructured successfully with domestic consumption and exports showing improvement in 2003. A number of global industries are now dominated by Korean enterprises, rather than the Japanese conglomerates.

- Asia's markets have outperformed the world in terms of productivity growth. Most Asian companies' deleveraging and restructuring led to greater improved performance than their counterparts in the United States and in Europe.

have few locally owned hedge funds firms. There are signs that this phenomenon is starting to change, which will be welcome as the advantages of local managers are obvious, in particular pertaining to language and contacts. However, it could be some time until the situation reverses. Hedge funds are entrepreneurial in nature, and certain systems in Asia do not cater to this. Japan, for example, is the most advanced hedge fund market in Asia. In some countries there are also structural barriers; Japan's cross-holdings culture, for example, has direct implications for the concept of shorting.

The Asian crisis of the late 1990s had a detrimental effect on the reputation of hedge funds in this region, since hedge funds were arguably perceived by many Asians to have been instrumental to the crisis. The near collapse of Long Term Capital Management (LTCM) in 1998, which had considerable investments in Asian markets, merely served to enhance this poor reputation. Prior to 1998 many Asian countries had exchange rates that were pegged to the U.S. dollar. During the early to mid-1990s, many of these currencies were technically overvalued. Hedge funds during the 1990s had a global macro bias; hence they sought to profit from anomalies on a macrolevel. A number of funds sought to aggressively short Asian values, on the basis of their being overvalued. Ultimately, the inevitable decline of these currencies was a fundamental part of the problems encountered by Asia during this time period.

The extent to which hedge funds actually can be held accountable for either causing or exacerbating the downturn of the Asian economies is, of course, questionable. Most commentators claim that they were merely used as scapegoats by governments that had mismanaged their economies. However, the perception of hedge funds by the Asian authorities and public alike will remain key to the actual level of growth of this industry within the region.

The mistrust of many Asian authorities toward hedge funds has manifested itself through the amount of legislation passed restricting onshore investing in such funds and the ability to operate a fund in an uninhibited manner. At present, a number of restrictions on shorting stock, an essential component of most funds' strategies, exist throughout the region. Nevertheless, the number of Asian-dedicated funds has increased dramatically over the last few years.

Perhaps the most important point to make at this stage is that the number of macro players in the region has reduced dramatically from pre-1998 levels, as the number of such funds has decreased overall and the perceived opportunities in the region are less. In addition, because of the LTCM debacle, investors are far less willing to consider funds with such an aggressive risk profile. Levels of leverage are lower, funds are taking a more responsible approach to asset growth, and transparency is, overall, much improved. It therefore can be argued that there is now much less reason for Asian authorities to fear the impact of a hedge fund blow-up on their economies. As to whether hedge funds represent an inherent threat to the financial stability of an economy, the contrary can be argued. Hedge funds are essentially risk takers and therefore providers of liquidity. In addition, the changed profile of hedge funds operating in Asian markets, in terms of strategy, leverage, and risk control, has significantly reduced the inherent risk that these funds represent to an economy's stability.

The issue of capacity is an even more critical issue in Asia, where liquidity is not as healthy as in the United States or Europe. This issue will increase in importance as assets continue to flow into Asian funds. One might therefore expect a hedge fund investing exclusively in Asia to close at a much lower level of assets than its U.S. or European counterparts, although the inclusion of Japan in the investable universe clearly will add substantially in terms of capacity.

Although the amount of capital allocated to Asian hedge funds has increased substantially in percentage terms, this demand has been outstripped by the increase in new funds opening. Further, there are huge discrepancies in the sizes of funds. Some managers are closed and turning away new money; others are struggling to reach even a moderate level of assets under management. In fact, a high percentage of funds have less than $50 million under management.

Renewed interest in the region has yet to capture major inflows or allocations, particularly for funds investing outside Japan. Japan-based managers have the highest levels of assets under management, and Singapore has the lowest.

Capacity is, in our view, more likely to be an issue for funds investing in Asia than for those investing in Europe, from the perspective both of the liquidity of the Asian markets and amount of hedge fund capital that can be invested without threatening returns and also regarding access to the best managers. However, these are longer-term issues, even assuming continuing rapid growth of assets under management; it will be some time before the level of assets managed by hedge funds will be sizable enough as a percentage of total assets for their actions to have a material market impact.

From various discussions with managers, we estimate that a responsible hedge fund manager for Asia without Japan (equity long/short) would look to close the fund at $250 million; for a Japan-only fund, this figure would be closer to $500 million.

Asia Hedge and the Bank of Bermuda have an Asian Hedge Fund Index that dates to the end of 2000. Although this is a relatively short period, this time frame is appropriate since the majority of Asian invested hedge funds have started up in the last two years. The index shows that Asian hedge funds clearly outperformed the markets during the period, by some margin. In addition, and perhaps more surprisingly, these funds generally have done a good job of protecting the downside.

Japan-only long/short managers are consistent performers and generally offer positive returns. Asia, including Japan managers, also had positive returns. Once again it is important to highlight the importance of selecting the right managers. Japan-only long/short managers have largely proven adept at protecting the downside, which is important when investing in Asia. As evidence, consider that in the bull market of 1999, there were funds that delivered positive returns as high as 250 percent or more, yet these funds suffered in the ensuing bear market. The net result was often positive, but, depending on the timing of the subscription/withdrawal, few investors benefited. Although some investors will be reluctant to return to Asian hedge funds after having experienced such volatility in the past, the recent performance of the strategy and the recognition that not all funds need be that volatile should encourage the continuation of the inflow of capital into Asian funds.

Another important consideration for Asian hedge funds is that in some Asian economies, shorting stock—a key element of an equity long/short or market-neutral fund—has not been permitted. In Korea and Taiwan, for example, managers cannot short stocks, but can short American Depository Receipts (ADRs), Global Depository Receipts (GDRs), and index futures. There have been indications that the authorities will move away from these restrictions, but this is not a certainty and the time frame is unknown. Yet hedge fund managers investing in Asia are confident that changes ultimately will be introduced that will enable them to operate more effectively in these markets.

In India, managers cannot short stock or index futures, but can short ADRs and GDRs. In Malaysia, managers cannot short stock but can short index futures. In Indonesia, none of these methods of hedging risk can be used. In Thailand, there is no restriction as such on shorting, but in practice it is not easy to do so, due to the difficulty in borrowing stock.

In Hong Kong, Singapore, and Australia, there is no problem in shorting stock. Investments in China are increasing, a trend that is expected to continue as the nation grows in importance. Many Chinese corporations have sought listings in Hong Kong and Singapore, and even in western markets.

Japan has long been one of the most attractive environments in Asia for hedge funds, not least due to the ability to borrow stock and take short positions. Some concern was expressed at the imposition by the Japanese authorities, in February 2002, of new restrictions on shorting stock, the main component of which was the imposition of the uptick rule (meaning that a stock can be shorted only after an upward move), which brings Japan in line with the United States and a number of other countries that have active and liquid stock borrow/shorting markets.

Thus far the impact has been negligible. The uptick rule will increase trading costs and thus could penalize high-turnover strategies including convertible bond (CB) arbitrage and hedging short gamma positions. More conventional naked shorts, though, are placed with the expectation of more than 50 percent potential returns and will not be deterred by the marginal inconvenience. The authorities are claiming with some justification that they are merely matching U.S. regulatory standards. Most managers have viewed the move as nothing more than an attempt to boost the market ahead of the March book-closing, a goal that was accomplished.

Hedge fund managers are not concerned by these regulations in themselves. What would present a problem, however, would be the imposition of further restrictions. The authorities have it in their power to do more serious damage. The most effective way would be to organize a sudden recall of stock from the borrowing market by major institutions. This scenario is widely regarded as unlikely.

On the upside, foreigners' ownership of the market is significant; therefore, the dependence on Japanese institutions is falling. And with one-year interest rates nearly at zero, the major domestic players are very grateful for the existence of stock borrowers.

One school of thought argues that the Japanese authorities have little appreciation of the importance of market efficiency and regulatory consistency, and that even at the highest level of the financial administration, there is deeply ingrained suspicion of hedge funds and relatively poor understanding of what they actually do. However, a sophisticated and intelligent market dialogue is present in Japan, and it is doubtful that the Japanese authorities would resort to measures that would make it difficult for hedge funds to operate in their markets. Thanks to Japan's structural current account surplus, its financial institutions always will be major players in global markets, particularly U.S. credit markets. Japanese investors are receptive to new ideas and currently eager to locate market-uncorrelated gains. In the medium term, rather than attempting to shut out hedge funds, Japan is more likely to try to develop its own hedge fund industry. Authorities across the region are likely to become more, rather than less, tolerant to the practice of shorting stock, as they become increasingly aware, through ongoing education, that hedge funds do not represent the threat to their financial stability that they may once have supposed.

Although the picture as a whole looks encouraging, it is possible that politically unstable countries such as Malaysia and Indonesia may not make much progress in this respect, since the development of financial markets is not high on the list of government priorities. However, as long as the key financial centers in Asia (Tokyo, Hong Kong, Singapore, Australia, and, increasingly, Shanghai) are developing the breadth and depth of the markets, the opportunity for hedge fund managers to operate efficiently in Asia will improve. Even less sophisticated markets, currently starved of foreign capital, are at the very least unlikely to impose further obstacles, as their authorities recognize the importance of attracting foreign investors back to their markets.

For fund of hedge funds (FOHF) and hedge fund managers looking to source capital from Asian investors, there have been some encouraging developments recently. Both the Singaporean and Hong Kong financial authorities have approved the controlled marketing/public offering of hedge funds.

Much of the consultation that was conducted prior to authorization addressed the subject of protecting retail investors. Even though hedge funds are generally more adept at protecting capital due to the tools at their disposal, the relative lack of transparency available from hedge funds meant the need for additional protection. With these regulations, the Hong Kong SFC has sought to balance the fairness and overall integrity of the markets while at the same time allowing the natural market forces to function effectively. In addition, the political ramifications of a hedge fund crashing and hurting Hong Kong investors would be dramatic. Hence the adoption of a market segmentation system that requires a relatively high minimum investment (US $50,000) for single-manager funds. The exception would be the FOHF products, with a minimum investment of $10,000, since FOHFs generally will reduce risk through diversification. Not surprisingly, there will be no minimum for capital-guaranteed hedge fund products.

The Hong Kong SFC also has imposed other restrictions, such as the requirement for hedge fund and FOHF managers offering hedge fund products to have US $100 million in assets under management and have a five-year track record.

In Singapore, the minimum investment is Singaporean $50,000. This is lower than in Hong Kong, and no distinction is made between hedge funds and FOHFs for this purpose. In addition, there is no minimum asset under management requirement for those offering the products, although a minimum five years' track record is mandatory.

These restrictions will limit the growth of hedge funds somewhat by excluding numerous potential buyers and suppliers of these products. This is why single hedge funds located in the region are unlikely to emulate the recent success of guaranteed products, at least in terms of the amount raised from the public. Another barrier will be that of educating investors about hedge funds. Doing so will require highly trained intermediaries, especially in banks, which are becoming the main centers of fund distribution.

Overall, however, there is essentially a positive step for the continued growth of the hedge fund industry in Asia. The restrictions imposed are not unreasonable, and the authorization of offering of such products should be viewed very favorably, given the historically cautious view taken by Asian financial authorities toward hedge funds. As education increases, the restrictions may be relaxed, which will spur further growth. In the meantime, most likely the main beneficiaries of this regulation will be established FOHF operators with reasonable assets and a sound track record. In several recent examples, managers have closed their funds within one year of starting to trade by raising up to $500 million of assets.

Hedge fund managers operating Asian strategies are very optimistic about the investment opportunities that they perceive to exist. As stated earlier, many managers see a huge anomaly between those companies that have made or are in the process of making the necessary reforms and whose stock is grossly undervalued and the converse situation where the stock valuations are being held up by the complex cross-shareholdings that remain in place.

Japan's managers are generally not concerned about the recent imposition of the uptick rule that relates to shorting in Japan. Most managers in this region are not very active traders. The small additional cost of stock borrowing brought about by the additional administrative burden will have negligible impact on overall returns. Regarding the rest of Asia, managers are fairly optimistic that existing restrictions on shorting will be relaxed in key markets, such as Korea and Taiwan.

Managers are still reporting a significant increase in overall investor interest in their funds, but not necessarily from Asian investors. For the most part, current investors in Asian hedge funds are based in Europe or the United States. Probably most of the increase in hedge fund investments by Asians in the near term will occur in hedge funds that are invested outside the region.

Next we turn to key factors that will drive the growth of the Asian hedge fund industry going forward.

ABILITY OF HEDGE FUNDS TO OPERATE EFFECTIVELY

An important component of a typical equity long/short or market-neutral hedge fund is the ability to take short positions in stock and thereby offset the risk inherent in the long positions. As noted, this is not possible in a number of Asian markets; some commentators are concerned that the recently imposed regulations in Japan, although not a hindrance in themselves, signal a more stringent regime in the future. The perceived ability of hedge fund managers to carry out their strategies while being able to effectively manage risk will be an important consideration for many investors when determining whether to allocate to Asian strategies.

Asian markets have long been viewed by investors as capable of delivering very attractive returns, but also being fraught with risk. Volatility in these markets historically has been higher than in the United States and Europe, and it is not uncommon to see very substantial market swings in either direction. In many cases the impressive returns from these markets in the late 1980s and early 1990s were more than wiped out by the turmoil of 1997 and 1998.

Investors need to become comfortable with the risk controls that managers have in place. In the United States and Europe, in many cases hedge fund managers have been able to produce healthy positive returns in both bear and bull markets. There will be more skepticism that the same is possible in Asia, due to the difficulty in shorting individual stocks in some markets. Although volatility of returns for average Asian managers is still significantly higher than for their U.S. or European counterparts, evidence is emerging of managers in Asia who can replicate the consistent positive return profile of European/U.S. investors. These factors are unquestionably part of the reason for the recent increased level of interest in investing in Asia.

Although the vast majority of investors in Asian hedge funds have come from the United States or Europe, Asian investors have been demonstrating an increased interest in hedge fund investing, and Japanese institutions have already made some large allocations. Most of these have gone to funds invested in the United States and Europe. The ongoing education of Asian investors about hedge funds is necessary, and recent regulatory measures in Singapore and Hong Kong will help in this regard. As Asians' comfort level with hedge funds increases, it can be expected that so will the inflows from the region into hedge fund products.

High-profile investments by Asians in hedge fund products, such as the Hong Kong Jockey Club allocation of $100 million to two FOHFs, will add impetus to the growth potential. The Hong Kong Jockey Club is viewed as a very conservative organization; its venturing into the world of hedge funds, albeit via a consultant, will surely send a message to other potential investors.

Conversely, it is surprising that demand from relatively few Asian high-net-worth individuals and families have invested in hedge funds. An increase in demand from this segment would be a major boost for the industry.

There are a number of positive trends, including the fact that structural imbalances are being addressed in many parts of the region. There remain concerns, however, that Asia still has much to do in terms of structural reform. However, the steps that have been taken to date are viewed very favorably, and investors have a renewed interest in the region. In Korea, for example, banks are now lending to consumers and smaller businesses, not just Chaebols conglomerates that historically have been very powerful in Korean industry) that were able to source capital even where there was no commercial reason for the lenders. The considerable corporate restructuring that has taken place in Japan over the last few years has led to many attractive opportunities in that country. Currencies are also viewed as being at more realistic levels.

The Asian economies as a whole are witnessing improved economic activity. As mentioned, China's role in Asia's economic progress going forward should not be underestimated. Many would argue that therefore it would be more appropriate to invest at this stage in long-only funds, rather than hedging away much of the positive performance. This would be a reasonable comment, but also fairly short term. Hedge funds investing in Asia have shown their ability to limit the substantial downside in equity markets in recent years, and in the long term investors will be better equipped to deal with the high volatility and ultimately produce superior risk-adjusted returns.

Finally, there is the increased interest in hedge funds as a whole. More and more investors in Europe, for example, are becoming comfortable with the concept of investing in Asia; regional accessibility is improving, with retail offerings and lower minimum investments. China's recent membership in the World Trade Organization means these markets are now open to outside investors, and the number of opportunities available to investors in the region has increased correspondingly. The downturn in equity markets on a global basis has made many investors question the wisdom of long-only mandates. Asian investments can, at the very least, provide good diversification benefits for a portfolio of funds.

The key question relative to Asian investors is whether their capital will end up in Asian funds or in U.S./European funds. Many believe that the initiatives in Singapore and Hong Kong primarily will benefit established, international funds of funds that most likely have a stable of managers in the United States and/or Europe where they have confidence and capacity. If this is true, the U.S./European hedge funds will benefit more from the expected inflow of capital than the Asian hedge funds.

It is not possible to give a precise estimate of the inflow of capital into Asia from outside the region through hedge funds, and vice versa. What is confirmed, however, is that there are significant inflows into Asian strategies and that the majority of this is capital sourced from outside the region. Conversely, the majority of capital being allocated from within Asia is finding its way out, into U.S. and European invested strategies. It is difficult to see this relatively balanced state of affairs as changing in the near term.

Will the Asian hedge fund industry continue to grow as the European hedge fund industry has over the last few years? The positive developments that are taking place indicate that as investors become more educated to the advantages of investing in hedge funds, there is no reason why this should not happen. In addition, many U.S./European investors are looking to allocate to Asia. The Asian hedge fund market has been referred to as being four or five years behind Europe. If the pace of change continues and Asian investors come to embrace hedge funds, the reality could be even more promising for the Asian hedge fund industry.

In conclusion, despite the history of hedge funds in Asia and the high volatility of Asian markets being viewed as obstacles to investing in the region, many positive developments make Asia more attractive as an investment location by hedge funds and make hedge funds more attractive as an investment vehicle to investors. As a result we see an increase in allocations from Asian investors to hedge fund products in general. The hedge fund industry in Asia is still immature, and there is every reason to believe that it will see strong growth. In the short to medium term, the most likely impediment to this growth would be a high-profile hedge fund blow-up. We feel that the risk of such an event is substantially lower than was previously the case due to the specific strategies, lower leverage, and superior risk controls of the funds operating in Asia today. In spite of the overall immaturity of the hedge fund market in Asia, we believe that it should see strong growth.

DRIVERS OF PROFIT

Inefficiencies

One of the things that distinguish Japan and Asia in general is that it is a relatively inefficient market; opportunities may be greater than in the more efficient European and U.S. markets. A consistent theme from Asian managers is that these inefficiencies and clear anomalies can be found throughout the markets, hence increasing the return potential.

Low Valuations

Although hedge funds aim to deliver positive absolute returns regardless of market conditions, the reality is that equity-based funds generally will perform better in upward-trending markets. Many Asian companies are still, in most managers' opinions, on very low valuations, and the potential for an improvement in these valuations is substantial, particularly with the positive economic outlook emanating from the reforms being put into place.

Country Selection

Outside Japan there is a lower correlation between the Asian markets than is the case in Europe, for example. Country allocations therefore can be an important determinant of return. (See Figure 12.1.)

DRIVERS OF RISK

Liquidity

It has been noted that Japan is favored over other Asian markets due to the higher level of liquidity in its markets. Most Asian markets have much lower levels of liquidity than their western counterparts. Liquidity is a very important consideration for hedge fund managers when managing the risk in their portfolios. Those managers who restrict themselves to relatively liquid securities will be limited in their choices for

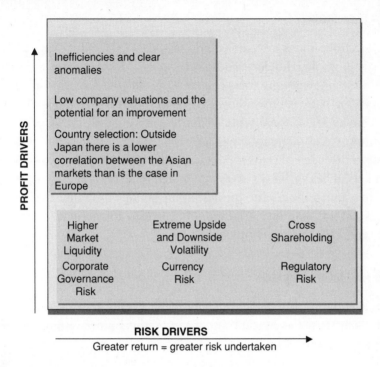

FIGURE 12.1 Key Drivers of Risk and Return in Asia.

long positions and even more so with short positions; long positions cannot always be hedged effectively, depending in some markets on the availability of ADRs and GDRs for particular stocks.

Volatility

The liquidity issue in Asia outside Japan is one of the key reasons for the volatility. Extreme upside and downside movements in very short spaces of time are not uncommon. This fact in itself brings a new dimension to risk management; stop losses, for example, can be ineffective in such an environment. Some managers have varying stop losses, based on historical short-term volatility, which is a sensible means of addressing the problem. This issue will remain a key one for managers going forward.

Cross Shareholding

Cross shareholdings are particularly prevalent in Japan, with banks the primary cross shareholders. The existence of cross shareholdings can have important implications for price movements; the situation may arise where a big bank is unwinding a position, and it is important that managers are aware of these types of issues and how they could affect their positions. Cross shareholdings have been used to determine value, but failed to provide either transparency or an accurate snapshot of a company's fiscal health. This system is expected to be reformed, which should lead to a much more efficient market in Japan. Assuming that reforms do take effect, liquidity also should be added to the market as banks unravel the existing structures.

Corporate Governance Risk

Although significant steps are being made in this area in a number of Asian countries, the concept of corporate governance barely existed in recent years and is still lagging compared to Europe and the United States. This fact provides an additional or at least enhanced risk of investing in the region.

Currency Risk

Investors looking at Asia should be mindful of currency risk and may consider accessing the market through a fund that hedges foreign exchange risk. Many hedge fund managers in Japan, for example, run identical strategies across two funds—one U.S. dollar-denominated and the other in yen.

Regulatory Risk

The regulatory environment is an additional issue and source of risk for hedge funds. Although we believe that this environment is more likely to improve than deteriorate, the possibility of further regulation that would hinder the ability of hedge funds to operate effectively in the region cannot be discounted altogether.

INDIVIDUAL STRATEGIES

Equity Long/Short

Equity long/short is the dominant hedge fund strategy in Asia currently. The key reason for this is that hedge fund managers perceive that significant inefficiencies exist in the equity markets and therefore there is potential for very substantial returns.

The issues that face managers of this strategy in Asia, particularly outside of Japan, have been discussed at length. In brief, these issues include difficulties in shorting in some markets, high levels of volatility, and, in many cases, poor liquidity levels. These factors add additional dimensions to risk management resulting in varied risk-adjusted returns. Despite the fact that many funds do not have long track records at this stage, the evidence suggests that some managers are adept at navigating these additional risks.

Market Neutral

A plethora of new managers have started market-neutral strategies, primarily in Japan. Market-neutral strategies purport to eliminate market risk altogether by fully offsetting long positions with short positions. There is no directional bias whatsoever, and the rationale for these strategies is that positive returns can be generated regardless of the general direction of the markets, through appropriate selection of positions. A key element of implementing such a strategy successfully is easy access to stock margin and a good level of liquidity, so that the cost of such borrow is not prohibitive.

Unlike most other Asian markets, the Japanese markets have characteristics that make the operation of a market-neutral strategy feasible. Indeed, the large number of inefficiencies that exist in Japan makes the strategy all the more attractive. One reason for the large number of inefficiencies is the relatively small number of arbitrage players operating in the Japanese markets.

Market-neutral funds that have recently started investing in Japan are primarily equity market neutral, but also include statistical arbitrage and derivative arbitrage.

Given the state of the Japanese economy/markets over the last decade, these low-risk strategies are expected to be appealing to Japanese and foreign investors alike.

Convertible Bond Arbitrage

The majority of convertible bond issuance historically has come from the United States and Japan. Japanese issuers generally have had better credit ratings than their U.S. counterparts, although this situation is changing somewhat as the creditworthiness of U.S. issuers continues to improve. Interest rates at close to zero have reduced the potential for static returns, but the long volatility strategies still can produce returns in the market.

The Nikkei historically has exhibited an average volatility that is higher than the Standard & Poor's, making it a fertile ground for arbitrage dealings. To help manage risk, arbitrageurs can stick to blue-chip names in Japan and forgo the weaker credits. Unlike the U.S. convertibles market, most returns in Japan are produced by delta trading (hedges on the underlying movement in price between the equity and bond). In U.S. or European markets, only around 20 percent of returns comes from delta trading. In the United States, managers are getting value from the actual coupon. In Japan, with interest rates being essentially zero, this is impossible.

Most bonds in Japan have call provisions, but it is very uncommon for the companies to call domestically issued paper even when it would appear to be beneficial to do so. One of the most important reasons for this is the complex cross-ownership of shares that exists. Shareholders would be the primary beneficiaries from a bond being called, since the probability of the option being exercised by the bank holders of shares and bonds would be low.

A number of convertible bond arbitrageurs offer Japan-only funds. As described, high levels of volatility and high credit quality issues have attracted these arbitrageurs to this market. The outlook, however, is not as positive. Recent trends have arguably made Japanese convertible bonds less attractive in relative terms than their U.S./European counterparts. For one thing, the credit quality of the issuance in the latter markets has improved. Also, and perhaps more important, issuance in Japan has declined and a number of existing issues are expiring, thereby reducing the overall liquidity of the convertible bond market. This situation is in stark contrast to the increase in new issuance that has occurred in Europe recently. There also has been an increase in convertible bond issuance in Asia outside of Japan, but that market remains secondary to the more liquid U.S. and European markets.

Merger Arbitrage/Event Driven

There are still relatively few event-driven and merger arbitrage funds in Asia. However, funds with a global mandate are increasingly interested in Asian opportunities. This situation is likely to increase going forward as the ongoing need for restructuring and trends in many industries toward consolidation make the outlook for participants of this strategy very attractive. Arguably, the case for restructuring is even stronger in Asia, especially in Japan. For this strategy, it is necessary to fully understand the relevant regulations and processes. The amount of knowledge required may keep some managers away in the short term, but the attraction of higher returns than for those markets in which many arbitrageurs already operate will almost certainly attract much attention once the inevitable restructuring picks up again. Expect dedicated funds to follow soon.

TIPS

The impressive rise in asset allocation to Asian strategies in the last several years is the combined result of Asian investors seeking access to absolute return strategies, of managers starting funds that focus on investing in the Asian markets, and of investors in general taking more interest in the investment opportunities available in Asia. Asian financial markets are not as efficient as the U.S. and European markets and therefore offer good investment opportunities. The hedge fund industry's growth in Asia is also the result of increased education throughout the region, which is a boon to the industry.

- Recognize that Japan-focused funds are the primary beneficiary of the actual inflow of hedge fund capital into the region because many fund managers have built up Japanese trading and language skills.
- Understand the impact of the recent restrictions on shorting stocks in Japan and the fact that it is still easier to short in Japan than in the rest of Asia.
- Know that there are few local managers in Asia and that more than half of the assets invested in Asian hedge funds are managed from outside the region, mainly from the United States.
- Expect a hedge fund investing exclusively in Asia to close at a much lower level of assets than its U.S. or European counterparts as a result of capacity and liquidity issues.
- Study size versus performance issues as a basis for an investment in the Asian region because there are huge discrepancies in the size of funds.
- Appreciate the importance of selecting the right hedge fund managers when investing in Asia.
- Monitor regulatory issues in Asia, particularly those relating to the shorting of stock.
- Watch for increased restrictions on hedge fund manager activity, which could be detrimental.
- Be extra careful if investing in politically unstable countries, such as Malaysia and Indonesia.
- Understand the key drivers of risk and return in Asia and how they impact investors.

CHAPTER 13

Hedge Fund Indices:
In Search of a Benchmark

Hedge fund indices are gaining more notoriety than ever as investors seek ways to benefit from the usefulness of an accurate benchmark by which to measure investment performance.

Just as a precise benchmark such as the Standard & Poor's (S&P) 500 has furthered the equity and mutual fund industries, an accurate index can do nothing but accelerate the growth of the hedge fund market. Although a lack of continuous and complete data prevents current hedge fund indices from being the equivalent of the S&P 500, they are still good tools for investors. Today's hedge fund indices show recent hedge fund performance within a small degree of error and help investors determine expectations of their own hedge fund investing experience. (See Table 13.1.)

Beginning in 2004, the *Wall Street Journal* began publishing several hedge fund strategy indices in an effort to capture performance. Additionally, many firms are establishing a presence either through their own proprietary set of indices or through a much-debated, passive investment approach. These indices, whether characterized as "investable" or "simple benchmarks," track either a specific fund style or the overall hedge fund market. Despite the many inconsistencies and biases associated with them, hedge fund indices have the ability to reasonably characterize the directionality of hedge fund performance. Relative benchmarks for hedge funds do make sense and should be utilized as a directional gauge. As the

TABLE 13.1 Hedge Fund Indices Performance in 2003

Index	2003 YTD Return
1. Hennessee H. F. Index	19.69%
2. HFRI Fund Weighted Composite Index	19.56%
3. Van U.S. Hedge Fund Index	19.00%
4. CSFB/Tremont Hedge Fund Index	15.44%
5. The Bernheim Index®	15.30%
6. MSCI Hedge Fund Composite Index	14.71%
7. EACM 100 Index	12.40%
8. S&P Hedge Fund Index	11.10%
9. InvestHedge Composite Index	9.28%

Disclaimer: The information and statements of facts in this table are based on sources LJH Global Investments, LLC believes to be reliable, but does not guarantee their accuracy. Options and estimates included in this article constitute the judgment of LJH Global Investments, LLC as of the date of publication and are subject to change without notice.

hedge fund market develops and transparency increases, it is likely that a practical benchmark will rise to become the industry standard.

At this time, hedge fund investors need to understand the utility of the existing hedge fund indices and the databases used to collect fund data. It is critical to be aware of the shortcomings associated with these indices, including data discrepancies and biases, construction methodologies, classifications, and the absolute return versus relative performance debate. It is interesting to compare and contrast each index provider with respect to construction methodologies and performance data, to explore the notion of "investable" indices, and to discuss the pros and cons of an active versus passive approach.

Finally, we consider the future of hedge fund indices in the context of recent trends in the hedge fund industry. Specifically, we examine the role that transparency and increased regulation will play on these indices and on hedge funds in general. Clearly, hedge fund investors can benefit from the usefulness of a relative benchmark. Although no universal hedge fund index can adequately represent the hedge fund world and although existing composites differ widely in composition and performance, hedge fund indices are still reasonably good indicators of performance. (See Table 13.2.)

TABLE 13.2 Hedge Fund Representative Indices

Hedge Fund Indices	Inception	Number of "Strategy" Indices	Classification Methodology	Selection/Sampling Criteria Examples	(Weighted/Simple) Mean vs. Median
HFR	1994	37	Classified by manager	No minimum time or AUM* Separate samples for offshore and onshore + combined one	Simple mean
Altvest	2000	14	Classified by Altvest	No minimum time or AUM* Include both onshore and offshore funds	Simple mean
Hennessee	1987	24	Classified by the manager and committee approved	Minimum AUM* of US$10mm 1 year	Simple mean
CSFB/Tremont	Nov-99	14	Classified by Tremont	1 year or $500mil AUM* Minimum $10mil AUM* Include both onshore and offshore funds	Asset weighted mean
S&P Indices	2002	10	Classified by S&P	Minimum AUM* and track record volatility screens	Simple mean
MSCI Indices	Jul-02	4: Further segment into 190 indices	Classified by the manager and committee approved	Includes all funds in universe Eliminates duplicates (onshore only)	Asset weighted & Simple mean
Dow Jones	2003	5	Classified by the manager and committee approved	Minimum AUM* & track record, due diligence, qualitative screens Each index is run as a managed account—essentially they are investable indices as well	NAV calculation (as an aggregate portfolio)
Van Hedge	1994	25	Classified by Van Hedge	No minimum track record or AUM*	Simple mean

*AUM = Assets under management

Disclaimer: The information and statements of facts in this table are based on sources LJH Global Investments, LLC believes to be reliable, but does not guarantee their accuracy. Options and estimates included in this article constitute the judgment of LJH Global Investments, LLC as of the date of publication and are subject to change without notice.

HEDGE FUND DATA AND DATABASES

In an attempt to monitor hedge fund performance, several hedge fund data vendors collect monthly performance figures for thousands of hedge funds. Also, some firms maintain their own databases from which to construct hedge fund indices. The typical hedge fund database collects performance figures for each fund on a monthly basis. There are two primary methods for data collection: analyst entry or manager entry. Two commercial databases, Altvest and Hedgefund.net, currently rely on manager entry; the rest use analyst entry, according to a study entitled "A Comparison of Major Hedge Fund Data Sources" conducted by Strategic Financial Solutions, a comprehensive software company.

The type of data provided by these various database vendors also should be taken into consideration. Databases contain both qualitative and quantitative information. Qualitative data for each fund includes fields such as assets under management, fee requirements, performance returns, legal structure, minimum investment, and investment style. The Strategic Financial Solutions study also showed that data quality among the various vendors differs. Discrepancies were discovered in mostly qualitative data fields, including minimum investments as well as entry/exit/lockup information.

Worth noting, subscribing to a database is a method by which hedge fund managers can demonstrate their performance to the industry and potentially obtain new investors. However, hedge funds are not obligated to report to any database. When funds falter, they may elect not to report. Likewise, when funds close to new investment, they may stop reporting. Clearly, hedge fund data (or the lack thereof) are among the key issues facing the reliability of hedge fund indices.

EXISTING HEDGE FUND INDICES

The first indices used to track hedge funds appeared in the 1980s, but most were begun within the last decade. Currently about a dozen firms produce a variety of hedge fund indices that track either a specific fund style or the overall hedge fund market. As opposed to the traditional equity market where many look to the S&P 500, no particular firm's set of hedge fund indices has been established as the industry's standard for fund performance. However, the indices are efficient enough to serve as a valuable tool for hedge fund investors. At the very least, current indices provide investors with a reasonable representation of performance for the hedge fund market and individual investing strategies.

The typical set of indices published by each firm is divided according to fund investment style. Hedge funds usually are divided into several broad categories of strategy and then classified according to more specific subtypes. Most firms producing indices have established an index for each classification of hedge fund they have identified. Through the use of these indices, investors can track with reasonable confidence the directionality of performance for funds adhering to certain styles of investing.

INVESTABLE INDICES

Another recent trend in the development of hedge fund indices is the inception of investable indices. These indices are essentially "tracking" portfolios following a passive investment approach. They seek to emulate the aggregate performance of individual hedge fund strategies through careful construction methodologies and analyses. The products are geared more toward institutional investors and provide a cost-effective way to gain access to hedge funds. Currently, only a handful of index providers offer investable hedge fund indices. Some of the more recent players in the arena include Standard & Poor's, Morgan Stanley Capital International Inc. (MSCI), and Financial Times Stock Exchange (FTSE) based in London.

There are many proponents of investable indices, yet critics argue that investable indices face the same inefficiencies associated with database-produced indices. (See Table 13.3.) As we detail later, investors should be aware of several shortcomings before choosing a hedge fund index.

TABLE 13.3   Investable Indexing: A Better Avenue for Investing?

Investable indexes promote these benefits:

- Faithful representation of target universe
  - Present an accurate, unbiased picture of the universe of funds it tracks
  - Define what it seeks to track
- Transparency
  - Constructed in a systematic and consistent way
  - Public, prespecified calculation methodology
  - Published constituents
- Accountability
  - Audited or overseen by independent entity

Critical questions to ask:

- Are they solid "passive" investment vehicles?
- Do they make sense versus "actively managed," tailored fund of hedge fund portfolios?
- Do the funds selected provide the representative selection of the hedge fund market?
- What is asset allocation structured to accomplish? Is it equal weighted?
- Can an investor be ensured of equal representation and not just chasing hot money?

KEY CONSIDERATIONS OF HEDGE FUND INDICES

Although the various indices represent the actual performance of hedge funds to a good degree, several drawbacks exist when these indices are considered as true benchmarks of industry-wide performance. Current indices are a good tool for the hedge fund investors to keep track of the general level of performance among funds, but the numbers used to calculate these indices come from various imperfect databases. Thus, a hedge fund investor should keep certain things in mind about indices before he or she accepts the indices' returns as wholly accurate.

Inconsistencies and Biases

Although databases contain a bounty of information on hedge funds, there are many discrepancies between the various databases. As noted, information on assets, fees, and returns varies among the databases. The most significant reason for the differences among databases is that hedge fund managers voluntarily submit their own performance figures. Some fund managers may report to only a certain database, while others may choose not to submit to any databases. Fund managers may or may not submit data on their fund based on the quality of its performance. Not only may the data be unreliable, but the performance figures in databases also tend to be untimely. Hedge fund managers report their performance on a monthly return basis, yet data submission can lag behind by several months. This makes for a stark difference from the continuous pricing information available for common stocks and even the daily updating of mutual fund values. In addition, the databases differ in the number of dissolved funds they contain, which leads to a distorted view (called survivor bias) of the true performance of the hedge fund market. A single centralized database containing accurate information on all active and inactive funds does not exist at this time.

Because a complete record of hedge fund performance data that go into indices is lacking, numerous biases are inherent to the method used to calculate indices from existing databases. Foremost among biases associated with hedge fund performance is the just-mentioned survivor bias, the tendency of databases to attempt inconsistently to present returns for funds that are still active, as opposed to funds that did not survive. As a result, a database usually does not end a period with the same funds with which it began. Hedge funds generally are deleted from databases for reasons such as being merged or liquidated, or for halting the reporting of performance data. Although some funds that stop reporting performance data do so because they are enjoying excess profits and do not want to attract new investors, it is generally accepted that most funds stop reporting because of poor returns or excess volatility. Thus, databases tend to be disproportionately comprised of funds that have managed a long track record due to strong returns. The results of indices calculated from these databases tend to have an upward bias due to the exclusion of the funds that did not survive. According to one study conducted at Duke University entitled "Performance Characteristics of Hedge Funds and Commodity Funds: Natural versus Spurious Biases," the positive effect of survivor bias on hedge fund returns is estimated to be roughly 2 to 3 percent.

Selection bias occurs in databases and indices because not all possible funds in the industry are included in a database or index. In essence, selection bias occurs when a database selects particular funds to include, or when a fund manager decides not to submit performance returns to certain, or any, databases. Although a large number of hedge funds are not represented in databases, it is estimated that selection bias does not significantly affect hedge fund performance returns. The reason is that fund managers are thought not to release performance numbers to databases because of two offsetting reasons. Some fund managers may not report to databases (1) because of their superior returns and (2) out of a desire to remain out of the public eye. Thus, the fund managers who do not report because of poor returns offset the strong performance of the other funds that do not submit data.

Another bias in index returns is instant history bias, which occurs when a new fund is added to a database. A new hedge fund usually operates for a period of time to establish a performance record before it begins to solicit new investors and market itself to databases. Once it is included in a database, it can upload its performance into the database for the time before it was accepted into the database. Resulting performance figures represent an investment that may not have been available to hedge fund investors over that period, and fund managers are also likely to include these performance numbers in the database only when they showed strong performance. A study at Case Western Reserve University estimated that instant history bias has a positive effect of close to 1 percent on returns calculated from databases.

Strategy Classification

One characteristic that varies widely from index to index is the classification of hedge fund styles. Although broad similarities exist among the indices' categorization of funds, the specific styles referred to in the different databases can vary greatly. For instance, one firm's set of indices is divided among 10 identified strategies, and another firm's set of indices is based on more than 30 identified strategies. Another problem confronting the use of categorized styles is the inability of outsiders to verify that a particular fund manager is adhering strictly to the investment style for which his or her fund is categorized. Hedge fund managers must be flexible in their investment choices, and it may be imprudent to believe that all funds in an index classified as a certain style invest purely along the lines of that style. Some indices classify a fund according to the style in which the largest percentage of its assets is invested; other indices use advanced statistical techniques, such as cluster analysis, to classify funds regardless of their stated strategy. Given the differences among the existing indices' classification of styles, it is safe to say that there are no universal categories by which to categorize hedge funds.

Construction Methodology

Another aspect by which the hedge fund indices differ is the methodology used to construct them. For the most part, indices use equal weighting of the included funds to calculate value. However, some indices use an asset-weighted method to calculate their value. As there are several accepted methods to calculate an index, it is not unusual for different indices to use different methods. For instance, the Dow Jones Industrial Average uses a price-weighted method while the S&P 500 uses an asset-weighted method. Investors should remain aware of the differences between the methods. In addition, the number of funds used in hedge fund indices varies greatly. Sets of indices may draw on as little as 100 funds to calculate performance; others may use well over 1,000 funds from a database to compute an index. Typical numbers of funds used to compute a specific style index range from about 20 to over 50 hedge funds. As a result, due to the discrepancies in the construction of existing hedge fund indices, no one benchmark can be used to measure hedge fund performance.

FUTURE OF HEDGE FUND INDICES

Several trends are causing the hedge fund industry to grow and evolve at a quick pace. Primarily, the recent increased popularity of hedge funds has triggered a significant capital inflow and prompted the creation of many new funds and products. As the equity markets have exhibited increased volatility in recent years, many new investors have searched out hedge funds to reduce the risk exposure of their portfolios. Among the new investors flocking to hedge funds are large institutional investors, such as pension funds and endowments.

Institutions have begun to place considerable weight in the industry either by ownership of hedge funds or by apportioning their clients' assets into hedge funds. Although the large inflow of institutional money may be a bonus to hedge fund managers, it promises to alter the face of hedge fund investing at the same time. Institutions, particularly those with a fiduciary responsibility, such as pension funds, require greater transparency than what traditionally has been expected of hedge funds before they invest huge amounts of capital. In addition to this pressure from potential investors for greater transparency, hedge funds are also feeling pressure from regulatory authorities and the Internet to increase their transparency. A growing number of Internet sites now report current information and performance figures for hedge funds. By being able to distribute information to the investing public instantly, the Internet is certainly working to increase the transparency of hedge funds. Because a lack of information is at the heart of the challenge facing hedge fund indices, increased transparency will undoubtedly serve to improve the reliability of indices and push them toward complete accuracy.

Index-based investing is a new development in the hedge fund industry. A variety of products have begun to develop, such as principal-protected notes, exchange-traded certificates, and swaps. Investors now can have index-based investments structured to fit their needs. Although index-based derivatives are still in their early stages, these new products may prove to be the new paradigm in hedge fund investing.

TIPS

Investors will continue to benefit from accurate benchmarks by which to measure hedge fund investment performance. Just as a precise benchmark, such as the S&P 500, has furthered the equity and mutual fund industries, an accurate index will accelerate growth in the hedge fund market.

- Work with your financial advisor to set realistic personal expectations for your hedge fund investments.
- Understand that a central database with accurate information on all active and inactive funds does not exist at this time.
- Monitor existing hedge fund indices to determine how they compare, but realize that data quality differs between indices.
- Check whether the index you are monitoring relies on manager entry or analyst entry, which provides a good frame of reference in evaluating data.
- Use the indices to track with reasonable confidence the directionality of performance for hedge funds in your portfolio.
- Realize that investable indices basically are tracking portfolios that follow a passive investment approach.
- Consider the numerous biases inherent in databases with respect to the method used to calculate indices. For example, survivor bias refers to the tendency of databases to present returns only for active funds.
- Be aware that there are different methods used to calculate indices, such as asset weighted, price weighted, and equal weighted.
- Use to your advantage the fact that hedge funds feel pressure from regulatory authorities and the Internet to increase their transparency.
- Evaluate whether new products, such as principal-protected notes, exchange-traded certificates, and swaps, can be structured to fit your unique investment needs.

Glossary

Accredited investor An individual (1) who has made $200,000 per year in income for the past two years and has a reasonable expectation of doing so in the future; (2) and spouse with aggregate income of $300,000 per year; or (3) with a net worth of $1 million or more, excluding home and automobile. Certain hedge fund structures require that investors be accredited.

Administrator A third-party service provider that maintains the books and accounting records for a fund, communicates with investors, processes and reconciles trades, and monitors all cash movements. An administrator also may review and pay invoices for fund expenses, prepare financial reports, calculate net asset value, and calculate fees payable to the various service providers.

Alternative investments The alternative investment universe consists of investments outside of the traditional market investments of publicly traded debt, equity, real estate, and oil and gas. It includes investments ranging from hedge funds and managed futures to venture capital, private placements, and leveraged buyout funds.

ADV A form that all Registered Investment Advisors must complete and file with the Securities and Exchange Commission, which collects the information for regulatory purposes, such as deciding whether to grant registration. Form ADV information about investment advisors and their business is available to the public through the SEC.

Alpha A numerical value indicating excess rate of return relative to a benchmark. As it applies to hedge funds, it is a manager's "value-added" in selecting securities.

Alpha confidence interval (95 percent)   The range within which the true alpha of the manager is estimated to fall, with 95 percent probability.

Absolute return strategy   An investment strategy with the objective of securing a stipulated level of return independently of a proscribed traditional stock or bond market index. The strategy targets an absolute return range, not returns relative to a predetermined index. This strategy is commonly used with hedge funds.

Annual return   The total percent return for the year.

Arbitrage strategy   An investment strategy that attempts to take advantage of temporary price discrepancies between securities by buying the cheaper one and selling short the more expensive one. The strategy usually is based on the use of historical relationships between instruments in different markets to predict future trends of movements in price.

Asset class   A broadly defined group of securities that have similar risk and return characteristics. Examples of asset class categories include equities, fixed income, and cash.

Asset allocation   The percentage allocation of an investor's total portfolio in different asset classes.

Average gain   A simple average (arithmetic mean) of the periods with a gain. It is calculated by summing the returns for gain periods (i.e., with returns greater than or equal to zero) and dividing the total by the number of gain periods.

Average loss   A simple average (arithmetic mean) of the periods with a loss. It is calculated by summing the returns for loss periods (i.e., with returns less than zero) and dividing the total by the number of loss periods.

Average return   A simple average (arithmetic mean) calculated by summing the returns for each period and dividing the total by the number of periods. The simple average does not take into account the compounding effect of investment returns.

Beta   A historical measure of an investment's sensitivity to market movements. By definition, the beta of the market (as measured by the benchmark) is 1.0. A beta of less than 1.0 indicates that the investment is less sensitive to the market; a beta of more than 1.0 indicates that the investment is more sensitive to the market. Generally, the higher the correlation between the investment and the market (as measured by R-squared), the more meaningful is beta. Because beta is based on measurements of past performance, it is not an indication of what the investment's performance will be in the future.

Beta confidence interval (95 percent)   The range within which the true beta of the fund is estimated to fall, with 95 percent probability.

Benchmark   A standard against which risk and return investment performance can be evaluated. Widely used equity performance benchmarks are the total return of the Standard & Poor's 500, the Russell 3000, and the Morgan Stanley Capital International (MSCI) Europe, Australasia, Far East (EAFE) Index. Different benchmarks are used for evaluating different asset classes or styles of investing.

Black-Scholes   The most widely used option-pricing model to date, developed by Fisher Black and Myron Scholes in 1973. To determine the fair market value of an option, the Black-Scholes option valuation model considers the security's price, the exercise price, the risk-free rate, the time to maturity, and the standard deviation of the underlying asset price.

Bottom-up investing   An approach to investing that bases investment selection on fundamental analysis of specific companies, rather than a top-down approach that centers on evaluation of economic trends. Bottom-up investing involves detailed company-specific analysis to arrive at investment decisions. Emphasis is placed on company fundamentals such as earnings, cash flows, financial ratios, price/earnings ratios, and others to determine the relative value of a stock.

Calmar ratio   The average annual return for a period of time divided by the maximum drawdown during that period.

Collateralized debt obligation (CDO/CBO)   An asset-backed type of securitization whereby the underlying portfolio is comprised of securities, collateralized bond obligation (CBOs), or loans, collateralized loan obligations (CLOs), or a mixture of both. CDOs fall into two main categories. In balance sheet CDOs, usually the seller is a financial institution selling to restructure a debt portfolio, possibly to free up loaning capacity or reduce their regulatory capital. In arbitrage CDOs, the goal is to purchase a portfolio that will act as collateral for a securitization with tranches for the various risk levels required by investors.

Collateralized mortgage obligation (CMO)   A pass-through security that aggregates a pool of mortgage-backed debt obligations. Homeowners' principal and interest payments pass from the originating bank or savings and loan through a government agency or investment bank, to investors, net of a loan-servicing fee payable to the originator.

Commodity futures trading commission (CFTC)   A regulatory agency that monitors commodity pool operators and commodity trading advisors.

Commingled pools   A pool of capital made up of several investors in a single or multimanager strategy. The opposite of a separate, managed account for a single investor. Usually structured to allow for lower minimum investments than a separate account.

Compound (geometric) average return   The geometric mean is the monthly average that assumes there is an equivalent rate of return for each month to arrive at the same compound growth rate as when using the actual month-to-month return data. The quarterly and annual compound returns are calculated using the monthly compound return solution.

Convertible bond arbitrage   An investment strategy whereby one is simultaneously long the undervalued convertible securities (bond or preferred stock) and short the overvalued underlying equities of the same issuer, thereby "working the spread" between the two types of securities. This is considered a relatively conservative, market-neutral strategy (low or no correlation to the market), with a medium-term investment period.

Convexity   Refers to the shape (i.e., degree of curvature) of the price/yield relationship in a fixed income instrument.

Correlation   A measurement of relationship between two variables. The correlation coefficient (r) shows if there is any correlation between an asset and the market. Perfect correlation is 1.0; 0.0 is absolutely no correlation; and -1.0 is a perfect negative correlation. Studies indicate that a correlation coefficient below 0.3 has no correlation to the market.

Cumulative dollar profit   The total profit/loss in dollars (in millions) from inception to the end of the year.

Derivatives   Financial instruments that "derive" value from related securities or a combination of securities. For example, an equity option derives its value from the underlying equity volatility. A convertible bond derives its value from the underlying or "related" equity value and the fixed income characteristics of the bond.

Discretionary trading   The use of fundamental analysis or computer systems or a combination of the two to identify profitable trades. In general, this tends to be the highest-risk and highest-return strategy within the universe of hedge funds, with concentrated positions held for very short periods of time. The main difference between this strategy and systematic trading is that the investment decision is not automated; the manager makes the final investment decision.

Distressed securities   The securities of companies undergoing corporate restructuring, usually bankruptcy or reorganization. Investors seek to buy company securities at a low price and resell when/if the company comes out of bankruptcy and securities appreciate. Securities can range from low-risk senior secured debt to high-risk common stock.

Distribution   The number of gaining or losing rolling periods divided by the total number of rolling periods. Percentages in the "gain" and "loss" columns will total 100 percent.

Domestic (onshore) fund   An unregistered investment entity that is formed in the United States and open to U.S. investors. The general partner typically acts as investment advisor and manages the fund in return for an advisory and performance fee. The fund typically is structured as a limited liability corporation or a limited partnership.

Drawdown   The cumulative loss from peak to trough for any given period. A drawdown is in effect from the time an equity retrenchment begins until ground has been recovered.

Down percentage ratio   A measure of the number of periods that the investment outperformed the benchmark when the benchmark was down, divided by the number of periods that the benchmark was down. A larger ratio indicates better risk-adjusted performance.

Due diligence   A sequence of actions taken by an investor to ensure the validity of a particular manager or strategy. Usually due diligence takes the form of several standard questions and site visits to investigate the quality, reputation, background, and adherence to stated manager style and strategy discipline.

Duration   A measure of the sensitivity of a bond's price to changes in interest rates.

Durbin-Watson   A measure of serial correlation between regression residuals. A Durbin-Watson statistic of 2.0 indicates no serial correlation; near 1.0 indicates high serial correlation; and near 3.0 indicates high inverse serial correlation. High serial correlation can mean that the R-squared of a regression is overstated because of a cyclical relationship between the manager's returns and those of the index.

DV01   Refers to a parallel shift in the interest rate curve, which states that the market instruments in the interest rate curve are bumped by 1 basis point.

EAFE® Index   An unmanaged index of over 1,000 foreign common stock prices and includes the reinvestment of dividends. The Morgan Stanley Capital International Europe, Australasia, Far East index tracks 20 developed stock markets outside of North America.

Efficient frontier   A graphical representation of both the level of risk and the level of return for any given asset or combination of assets.

Emerging market   The market in any country with per capita gross national product of less than US$7,620 in 1990 (e.g., Russia, India, etc.) (according to the World Bank). This is primarily a long strategy, as many countries do not permit shorting. The holding period is usually short to medium term. Because these markets are less mature with high, volatile growth and inflation, expected volatility can be very high.

Equity market neutral   An investment strategy where an equal dollar amount of securities are held both long and short. The portfolio thereby theoretically maintains a neutral exposure to the market. If longs selected are undervalued and shorts overvalued, there should be net benefit. There are many variations on this basic structure: dollar neutral or equal dollars long and short; sector neutral with balanced sector weightings on both sides, and beta neutral.

Event-driven/opportunistic   An investment strategy that seeks to profit from special situations or opportunities to capitalize on price fluctuations or imbalances. Various styles or strategies may be employed simultaneously, or the strategy may be changed as deemed appropriate (e.g., there is no commitment to any particular style or asset class).

Fixed-income arbitrage An arbitrage that takes advantage of mispricing and distortions in value between two securities. Arbitrage profit opportunities often exist because different participants have different objectives, constraints, market outlook, and skill level. Yield spreads between fixed-income securities often provide arbitrage opportunities as market factors influence these relationships and produce value distortions. Various fixed-income instruments, such as Treasury bonds, corporate bonds, mortgage backed securities, and derivatives, are utilized in an arbitrage situation.

Fundamental investment analysis Analysis that is company specific and often includes a focus on earnings, dividends, and cash flow prospects. Consideration also is given to future interest rates and a risk evaluation of the company.

Fund of funds (FOF) A fund that invests in a portfolio of hedge funds. The fund's portfolio may utilize a variety of investment styles, thus creating a diverse vehicle for investors. The benefits of a FOF include: professional management and monitoring, lower minimums, extensive due diligence prior to investments being made, and access to investment managers that may not be available otherwise.

Geometric average return *See* Compound (geometric) average return.

Global macro fund An investment strategy that is primarily an opportunistic top-down approach, based on shifts in global economies. Hedge fund managers that specialize in this strategy base their investment decision making on economic outlook and speculate on changes in countries' economic policies, changes in currency and interest rate, and mispricing in general. The use of derivatives and leverage is not uncommon.

Growth/aggressive growth This strategy refers to investment in companies and industry groups expecting above-average growth in both revenue and earnings. Generally these have high P/E, low/no dividends and are usually small-cap or micro-cap stocks. Investments are normally hedged by shorting and/or options, and moderate volatility may be expected.

General partner The party with the general responsibility and liability for a particular limited partnership or other private placement vehicle.

Hedge funds A subset of the alternative investment asset class. The term usually refers to private investment vehicles that may utilize a wide range of investment strategies and instruments. Hedge funds include traditional stock and bond investments, but generally combine these with short sales, arbitrage, and leverage, strategies not generally used with traditional stock and bond market strategies. Normally they are structured as limited partnerships, limited liability companies (LLCs) or offshore investment companies where the general partner receives an incentive fee.

Hedge ratio   The number of stocks required to hedge against the price risk of holding an option or convertible security.

Hedging   A strategy designed to reduce investment risk using call options, put options, short selling, or futures contracts. A hedge can help lock in existing profits, and its purpose is to reduce the potential volatility of a portfolio by reducing the risk of loss.

High water mark   A loss carried forward. That is, if an investor makes $100 the first year and $100 the second year, then loses $100 in the third and fourth years, he or she is not really even. The general partner must make back the initial $200 gain before becoming eligible again for a performance fee.

Hurdle rate   The minimum investment return a fund must exceed before a performance allocation/incentive fee can be deducted. Frequently, London Inter-Bank Offer Rate (LIBOR), Treasury bills, a certain percentage, or other benchmarks measure this rate.

Incentive fees   Fee charged by the manager in addition to the management fee; it equals a percentage of profits, typically 20 percent, collected either on a monthly, quarterly, or annual basis.

Index   A number calculated by weighting prices or rates for a selected set of assets according to a set of predetermined rules (i.e., the Standard & Poor's 500 Index). The purpose of the index is to provide a single number that represents the market movement of the class of assets it represents.

Information ratio   The active premium divided by the tracking error. This measure explicitly relates the degree by which an investment has beaten a benchmark to the consistency by which the investment has beaten that same benchmark.

Interest only (IO)   A security representing the coupon payments from an underlying pool of mortgages. IOs are sold at a deep discount to their notional principal amount. The primary risk is early principal prepayment, thereby eliminating interest payments.

International/global   A strategy normally relying on both individual stock selection and general economic analysis of world markets. It entails investing in countries other than one's own domestic country, to benefit from other markets and provide diversification.

Jensen Alpha (Jensen A)   Quantifies the extent to which an investment has added value relative to a benchmark. It is equal to the investment's average return in excess of the risk-free rate minus the beta times the benchmark's average return in excess of the risk-free rate.

Kurtosis   Measures the flatness of the tails of any investment distribution. A flat-tailed distribution has an increased chance of a large positive or negative realization. Kurtosis should not be confused with skewness, which measures the flatness of one tail. Kurtosis sometimes is referred to as the volatility of volatility.

Leverage   The practice of borrowing to add to an investment position when one believes that the return from the position will exceed the cost of borrowed funds. Both institutional and individual investors can use leverage. Hedge fund managers often utilize leverage in order to increase returns. Leverage can magnify returns as well as losses.

Leveraged bond fund   An investment strategy designed to profit primarily from principal appreciation by utilizing leverage to purchase government bonds and, to a lesser extent, fixed-income derivatives. The holding period is normally short to medium term, and low volatility may be anticipated.

Limited partners   Usually investors in a limited partnership with no management activity or responsibility. The liability or risk is limited to the amount of invested capital; no personal assets are at risk. A limited partner has limited liability.

Liquidity   The ease of converting an invested asset to cash or liquid capital. Lack of liquidity can limit an investor regarding the timing of withdrawals from a particular account or strategy. For example, an investor may have to give 45 days' notice to withdraw cash from a particular investment vehicle.

Liquidity premium   An extra component of yield or return required to compensate the investor for the possibility that an adequate retail market may not develop for a security.

Long/short equity   A directional investment strategy that involves equity-oriented investing on both the long and short sides of the market. The objective is not to be market neutral. Managers can shift from value to growth, from small to medium to large capitalization stocks, and from a net long position to a net short position. Managers may use futures and options to hedge. The focus may be regional, such as long/short U.S. or European equity, or sector-specific, such as long and short technology or healthcare stocks. Long/short equity funds tend to build and hold portfolios that are substantially more concentrated than those of traditional stock funds.

Managed futures   An investment strategy that invests in listed financial and commodity futures markets and currency markets around the world. The managers are usually referred to as commodity trading advisors (CTAs). Trading disciplines are generally systematic or discretionary. Systematic traders tend to use price and market-specific information (often technical) to make trading decisions, while discretionary managers use judgment.

Management fee   A fee collected by the manager that typically offsets any fund expenses. The fee is usually asset based and is, on average, 1 percent collected on a monthly, quarterly, or annual basis.

Margin purchase   Securities purchased using money borrowed from a broker/dealer using other securities as collateral; a form of leverage.

Market neutral   An investment strategy that is intended to be "neutral" to traditional market volatility. The strategy seeks to provide a stated or absolute return rather than to outperform a traditional market index. The goal is to attain the target return regardless of broad market direction.

Market timing   A top-down investment strategy that shifts capital from one asset class to another, profiting from movements in interest rates and equity markets. It usually involves large commitments to one or more asset classes depending on the economic or market outlook, with a portfolio frequently being invested 100 percent in stocks, bonds, or cash equivalents. The strategy is based on anticipating the timing of when to be in and out of markets.

Mark to market   An accounting procedure required to maintain the credit balance in the short account equal to the market value of the short positions. When securities are sold short, they are placed in a short account within a general margin account. The resulting credit balance is isolated within the short account and adjusted weekly by the brokerage firm by a process called "marking to the market."

Maximum annual drawdown   The maximum percentage decrease from an equity high to an equity low for the year.

Multistrategy   An investment strategy that involves utilization of several distinct strategies, such as growth, risk arbitrage, and macro, in an effort to gain increased diversification. Funds of funds are typically multistrategy.

Net asset value (per share) (NAV)   The market value of a fund share. It equals the closing market value of all securities within a portfolio plus all other assets, such as cash, subtracting all liabilities (including fees and expenses), and then dividing the result by the total number of shares outstanding.

Net market exposure   The amount of a portfolio exposed to market risk because it is not matched by an offsetting position. It typically refers to the net difference between net long positions and net short positions. For example, a portfolio that is 100 percent long and 60 percent short has a net market exposure of 40 percent.

Offshore hedge fund   An unregistered investment fund domiciled outside the United States and open only to non-U.S. investors or U.S. tax-exempt accredited investors. Because of privacy and tax advantages, Bermuda, the Cayman Islands, and other international tax havens are popular domiciles for offshore funds.

Percent gain ratio   A measure of the number of periods that the investment is up divided by the number of periods that a given benchmark is up. A high ratio indicates desirable performance.

Preferred return   *See* Hurdle rate.

Prime broker   An intermediary that works closely with investment managers, investors, and third-party service providers (i.e., administrators), providing a vast array of essential services such as trade settlement, capital introduction, trade custody and reporting, and other margin lending activities, such as cash and/or stock lending to support leverage and short selling.

Principal only (PO)   A zero-coupon mortgage-backed security. POs are sold at deep discount to face value. They pay no periodic coupon interest. Principal is returned in the form of scheduled amortization and prepayments.

Private equity   Any investment strategy that involves the purchase of equity in a private company. These strategies include leverage buyouts, venture capital investments, distressed debt investments, and mezzanine debt investments.

Private placement memorandum   Also known as the Reg D private placement document or "offering memorandum." A document that outlines the terms of securities to be offered in a private placement. Resembles a business plan in content and structure.

Qualified purchaser   As defined in Section 2(a)(51) of the Investment Company Act of 1940, an individual with a $5 million investment portfolio or an institution with a $25 million portfolio. Certain hedge fund structures require that the investors be qualified purchasers.

Rate of return   Percentage appreciation in market value for an investment security or security portfolio.

Redemption   Partial or whole liquidation of interests in an investment fund.

Redemption fee   Fee charged upon a voluntary redemption from an investment vehicle.

Redemption notice period   Required notification period of an intended redemption request. Notification in writing usually is required.

Regional   An investment strategy in which investments are focused on specific regions of the world, such as Latin America, the Pacific Rim, and Europe.

Regulation D   A regulation adopted by the Securities and Exchange Commission under provisions of the Securities Act of 1933. Under Regulation D, many issuances of equity securities are exempt from registration with the SEC. This regulation saves private investment partnerships a significant amount of time and money in the process of raising funds.

Real Estate Investment Trust (REIT)   Created by Congress in 1960. A REIT is a company dedicated to owning and usually operating income-producing real estate such as offices, warehouses, apartment buildings, and shopping centers. To qualify as a REIT, an entity is legally required to pay virtually all of its taxable income to its shareholders every year.

Return/beta   The annual return divided by the estimated beta of the manager or index. It indicates how much return has been generated per unit of risk as defined by beta.

Return/standard deviation   The annual return divided by annualized standard deviation. It indicates how much return has been generated per unit of risk as defined by standard deviation.

Risk   Exposure to uncertain change, upside (positive change), or downside (negative change). Many types of risk are associated with investments (e.g., market risk, political risk). Many statistical measures, such as standard deviation, are used to understand and estimate risk associated with investments.

Risk-adjusted return   Investment performance adjusted for the level of risk that the strategy is exposed to. Usually risk is measured by standard deviation or the volatility demonstrated by the strategy. Typically, investments showing high return will have an increased level of volatility or a higher standard deviation.

Risk arbitrage   An investment strategy in which a long position is taken in the stock of a company being acquired in a merger or takeover and a simultaneous short position is taken in the stock of the acquiring company. Returns are produced from the inequality of stock prices from announcement date of the merger until the transaction closes. Often risk is reduced by avoiding hostile takeovers and investing only in deals that are announced. Medium volatility may be expected.

Risk premium The extra rate of return required to attract investors to an asset due to the incremental risk incurred from investing in it.

Rolling rate of return The average return of a rolling performance period.

R-squared (coefficient of determination) A measure of how well a regression line fits the data. It indicates the percent of variation in the data that is explained by the regression line. *R*-squared can vary between 0 and 1, where 1 indicates that 100 percent of the variation in the investment returns (dependent variable) is explained by the regression for the period measured.

Russell 1000® Index An index consisting of the 1,000 largest companies in the Russell 3000 Index, representing 89 percent of the total market capitalization of the Russell 3000.

Russell 2000® Growth Index An index containing those Russell 2000 securities with a greater-than-average growth orientation. Securities in this index generally have higher price-to-book and price-to-earnings ratios than those in the Russell 2000 Value Index.

Russell 2000® Small Stock Index An index comprised of the 2,000 smallest securities in the Russell 3000 Index, and includes reinvestment of dividends. It represents approximately 7 percent of the Russell 3000.

Russell 2000® Value Index An index containing those Russell 2000 securities with a less-than-average growth orientation. Securities in this index generally have lower price-to-book and price-to-earnings ratios than those in the Russell 2000 Growth Index.

Russell 3000® Index An index that measures the performance of the 3,000 largest U.S. companies based on total market capitalization, which represents approximately 98 percent of the investable U.S. equity market.

Sector funds An investment strategy that takes long and/or short positions in the companies of specific sectors of the economy, such as biotechnology, financials, and information technology.

Sharpe ratio A ratio calculated by subtracting the risk-free (Treasury bill) rate from a portfolio's total return and then dividing this by its standard deviation. Because the numerator is the portfolio's risk premium, the resulting fraction indicates the risk premium return earned per unit of total risk. It measures the reward-to-risk efficiency of an investment.

The Sharpe ratio seeks to measure the total risk of the portfolio by including the standard deviation of returns rather than considering only the systematic risk by using beta. In general, a higher Sharpe ratio suggests stronger risk-adjusted performance.

Short only An investment strategy based on the sale of securities that are overvalued from either a technical or a fundamental viewpoint, normally used when a bear market is imminent. The investor does not own the shares sold. They are borrowed from a broker, in anticipation of the share price falling and that shares can be bought later at a lower price and then can replace those borrowed earlier from the broker. Expected volatility may be very high.

Short selling The practice of borrowing a stock on collateral, immediately selling it on the market with the intention of buying it back later at a lower price.

Special situation An investment strategy that focuses on investing in companies that will or are undergoing events that will affect the price of a stock. An example would be a merger, spin-off, or restructuring.

Standard & Poor's 500 Index (S&P 500®) A registered trademark of The McGraw-Hill Companies, Inc., and has been licensed for use by Fidelity Distributors Corporation and its affiliates. It is an unmanaged index of the common stock prices of 500 widely held U.S. stocks. Standard & Poor's (a unit of The McGraw-Hill Companies, Inc.) calculates the market prices of these stocks, including the reinvestment of dividends, as a way to track the performance of the stock market in general.

Standard & Poor's Midcap 400 Index (S&P 400) A market capitalization-weighted index of 400 medium-capitalization stocks.

Standard deviation A statistical measurement of the dispersion about a fund's average return over a specified time period. It describes how widely returns vary over a designated period. Investors may examine historical standard deviation in conjunction with historical returns to decide whether a fund's volatility would have been acceptable given the returns it would have produced. A higher standard deviation indicates a wider dispersion of past returns and thus greater historical volatility. Standard deviation does not indicate how the fund actually performed, but merely indicates the volatility of its returns over time.

Statistical arbitrage   A market-neutral relative value investment strategy that attempts to profit from pricing inefficiencies. It involves the utilization of a quantitatively based investment methodology to identify securities or groups of securities that are currently trading at prices out of their historical range. The strategy involves establishing a long position in an undervalued security and short selling an overvalued security.

Stock index arbitrage   An investment strategy that involves buying a "basket" of stocks and selling short stock index futures contracts or vice versa.

Stock lending   A loan of a security from a legal holder to a borrower. The borrower uses the stock as their own, but remains liable to the loaner for all benefits the stock may produce, such as dividends. Stock lending began as a way to cover short sales, but has evolved and is incorporated into many hedge fund trading strategies.

Systematic trading   The method of seeking to identify a trend or pattern and position to stay invested as long as it persists. Systematic trading differs from statistical arbitrage in that each position is essentially an independent directional trade that is intended to produce a profit, not a relative position.

Top-down investing   An approach to investing in which an investor first looks at trends in the general economy and next selects industries and then companies that should benefit from those trends.

Tracking error   Indicates the degree to which a manager deviates from index returns. Tracking error is measured by taking the square root of the average of the squared deviations between the investment's returns and the benchmark's returns. A tracking error of 2 percent or less tends to indicate that the portfolio will perform similar to the index. A tracking error of 3 percent or higher, indicating that the portfolio deviates considerably (either favorably or unfavorably) from its benchmark index, is considered to be more actively managed.

Transparency   Literally, the state of being easily detected or seen through, readily understood, or free from pretense or deceit. In investing, it refers to the investor's ability to look through a hedge fund to its investment portfolio to determine compliance with the fund's investment guidelines and risk parameters.

Treynor ratio A ratio similar to the Sharpe ratio, except that it uses beta as the volatility measure (to divide the investment's return over the risk-free rate).

Up-capture ratio A measure of the investment's compound return when the benchmark was up divided by the benchmark's compound return.

Up-percentage ratio (UP %) A measure of the number of periods that the investment outperformed the benchmark when the benchmark was up, divided by the number of periods that the benchmark was up. A high ratio indicates superior performance.

Value An investment strategy based on acquiring out-of-favor securities whose prices do not yet reflect the companies' intrinsic value and/or are "underfollowed" by analysts. Normally asset, cash flow, and book value based are used to assess value.

Venture capital An investment in a start-up business that is perceived to have excellent growth prospects but does not have access to capital markets. It is a type of financing sought by companies seeking to grow rapidly and which are willing to exchange cash for equity.

Volatility The measure of the degree of dispersion of returns around the mean. Standard deviation is used as a statistical measure of volatility. Volatility is one of several investment risks.

Wilshire 5000 Index An unmanaged, market capitalization–weighted index of approximately 7,000 U.S. equity securities.

Within the hedge Describes an equity hedge portfolio in which long positions are matched by equal dollar amounts of short positions.

Wrap An investor can "wrap" a hedge fund investment with a private placement variable life insurance or annuity contract, eliminating the tax burden that frequently accompanies this style of investing.

Year-end VAMI (Value Added Monthly Index) The value that $1,000 invested at inception would be worth at the end of the calendar period.

Yield (internal rate of return) The percentage rate of return paid on an investment in the form of interest or dividends.

About the Authors

James R. Hedges IV is one of the early leaders in the hedge fund industry. He is the founder, president, and chief investment officer of LJH Global Investments, LLC, a hedge fund advisory firm based in Naples, Florida, with offices in London and New York.

Mr. Hedges is the most often quoted expert on hedge fund investing in the world and is often cited in financial publications including *Forbes*, *Institutional Investor*, the *New York Times*, *Barron's* and the *Wall Street Journal*, and appears regularly on CNN, CNBC, and Bloomberg. He also is on the Advisory Board of *The Journal of Wealth Management*, published by *Institutional Investor*, is a member of the Foundation for Fiduciary Studies and Lexington's *Who's Who*, and is an honorary member of The Foreign Correspondents Club.

More than a decade ago, Mr. Hedges set out to develop a hedge fund specialty firm that would meet the unique investment requirements of wealthy individuals and families, their advisors, and institutions. His vision focused on helping investors benefit from tailored hedge fund portfolios that would capture the opportunities presented by dynamic market conditions. Creating what rapidly has become a leading global hedge fund advisory firm required a commitment to diversification, capital preservation, and strong risk management capabilities.

Under Mr. Hedges's leadership, LJH's mission has been to provide access to top hedge fund managers who are subject to rigorous due diligence by LJH's team of hedge fund research analysts. The LJH organization also includes professionals in client development, sales force training, client service, and operations/reporting. The firm's expertise is

217

recognized by financial service firms such as banks, asset management firms, and insurance companies that rely on the firm as a subadvisor to build, manage, and service fund of hedge funds products. Also, LJH provides fund of hedge funds products for direct distribution to qualified investors.

Mr. Hedges graduated from Woodberry Forest School in 1985 and from Rhodes College in 1989 with a dual Bachelor of Arts in French and International Studies. Following an internship at the Chicago Board of Trade, Mr. Hedges earned a Master of International Management with a focus on Finance from the American Graduate School of International Management at the Phoenix, Arizona, Thunderbird campus.

From 1991 to mid-1992 Mr. Hedges lived in Paris and served as director of European Sales for J.D. Honigberg International, a Chicago-based global trading firm. Prior to founding LJH Global Investments, Mr. Hedges founded and served as managing general partner for Challenger Capital Management, L.P., a multimanager private family partnership investing in various alternative investments. Concurrently, Mr. Hedges was associated with the economic research and consulting firm of A. B. Laffer, V. A. Canto & Associates in La Jolla, California.

In 2002 Mr. Hedges attended the World Economic Forum in New York. He also has participated in The Wharton/Spencer Stuart Directors' Institute and Directors' Forum at The Wharton School of The University of Pennsylvania in 1997, The Program on Negotiation at Harvard Law School in 2001, and seminars at The Aspen Institute in Aspen, Colorado. He is currently a nonexecutive director of The Capital Markets Company ("Capco") in Antwerp, Belgium, Chairman of the Investment Committee of Attica—LJH Investment Management, Ltd., Chairman of LJH Financial Marketing Strategies, and a member of the S3 Asset Management Advisory Board. He has passed the NASD Series 2, 3, 7, and 63 exams.

The Securities and Exchange Commission invited Mr. Hedges to participate in its two hedge fund industry roundtables. Additionally, he was the first fund of hedge funds expert ever invited to speak to the Bank of Japan's executives, and he speaks frequently at leading wealth management and investment industry conferences.

Named in 2001 by *Art and Antiques* magazine as one of "the Top 100 Art Collectors in America," Mr. Hedges is an active supporter of the visual arts around the world. He is chairman of The Aspen Art Museum's National Council, a member of the Aspen Institute Art Gallery Advisory Board, and a director of the Dia Center for Arts in New York, The Drawing Center in New York, and ArtPace in Texas. He also serves on The Tate Gallery's International Committee. Mr. Hedges is also president of The Hedges Family Charitable Foundation.

Stuart Feffer and Christopher Kundro are managing directors and co-practice leaders for the Wealth & Investment Management practice at BearingPoint, a publicly traded management and technology consulting firm. They are responsible for developing BearingPoint's thought leadership with respect to private banking, wealth management, retail brokerage, asset management, as well as service-related businesses such as prime brokerage, fund administration, custody, and correspondent clearing.

Before BearingPoint, Mr. Kundro was a partner at Capco (The Capital Markets Company) and cohead of the firm's global Private Client & Asset Management practice. Before BearingPoint, Mr. Feffer was also a partner at Capco (The Capital Markets Company) and cohead of the firm's global Private Client & Asset Management practice. He has a PhD from the University of California-Berkley and a BA from the University of Chicago.

Index

References to figures are indicated by an "f" added to the page number. References to tables are indicated by a "t" added to the page number.